SRA

Reading Mastery

Signature Edition

Language Arts Teacher's Guide
Grade 2

Siegfried Engelmann
Karen Lou Seitz Davis
Jerry Silbert

McGraw Hill **SRA**

Columbus, OH

SRAonline.com

 SRA

Send all inquiries to this address:
SRA/McGraw-Hill
4400 Easton Commons
Columbus, OH 43219

ISBN: 978-0-07-612568-5
MHID: 0-07-612568-8

1 2 3 4 5 6 7 8 9 10 BCM 13 12 11 10 09 08 07

The **McGraw-Hill** Companies

Contents

PROGRAM ORGANIZATION

SCOPE AND SEQUENCE CHART, Part 1, Lessons 1–65

Lessons	1	5	10	15	20	25	30	35	40	45	50	55	60	65
REVIEW	██████████													
CLASSIFICATION AND CLUES	██													
SENTENCE CONSTRUCTION	████████████													
DIRECTIONS—North, South, East, West		██												
DIALECT														
Correcting		████████████████████████████████████												
Creating/Discriminating		██												
DEDUCTIONS		██											
PERSPECTIVE														
Relative Size			█████████											
Relative Direction							███████████████████████					
TEMPORAL SEQUENCING						████████████████████████████████					
CLARITY														
Correcting Ambiguity							██████████████████████████				
Creating Ambiguity										████████████		
Discriminating									██████████████			
REPORTING												████████	
STORY GRAMMAR														
Model Stories	██													
Application	██													
Extrapolation						█████████████████████████████					
Sentence Construction and Writing	██													
Alphabetizing							■ ■ ■					
Letter Writing											■		■

SCOPE AND SEQUENCE for Grade 2 Language Arts, Lesson 66–110

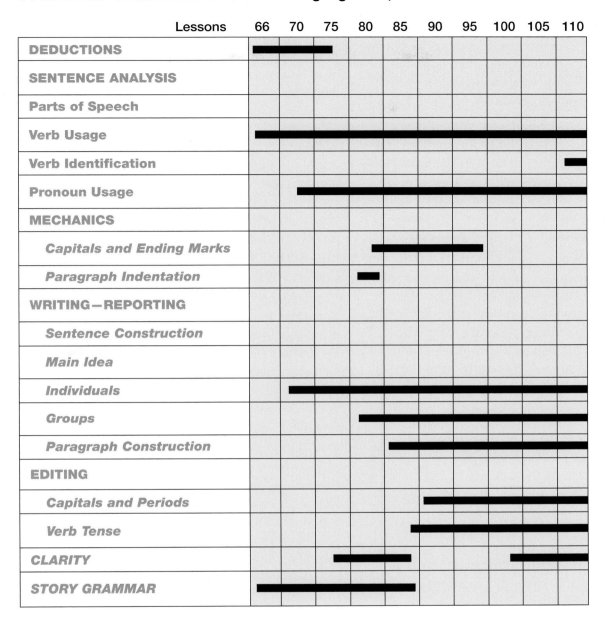

Lessons	66	70	75	80	85	90	95	100	105	110
DEDUCTIONS	▬	▬	▬							
SENTENCE ANALYSIS										
Parts of Speech										
Verb Usage	▬	▬	▬	▬	▬	▬	▬	▬	▬	▬
Verb Identification										▬
Pronoun Usage			▬	▬	▬	▬	▬	▬	▬	▬
MECHANICS										
Capitals and Ending Marks				▬	▬	▬	▬			
Paragraph Indentation				▬						
WRITING—REPORTING										
Sentence Construction										
Main Idea										
Individuals			▬	▬	▬	▬	▬	▬	▬	▬
Groups				▬	▬	▬	▬	▬	▬	▬
Paragraph Construction					▬	▬	▬	▬	▬	▬
EDITING										
Capitals and Periods						▬	▬	▬	▬	▬
Verb Tense						▬	▬	▬	▬	▬
CLARITY			▬	▬	▬			▬	▬	
STORY GRAMMAR	▬	▬	▬	▬	▬					

The scope and sequence charts on pages 4–5 show the organization of the Grade 2, Language Arts program. The program is divided into two parts. The first part (lessons 1–65) focuses on a variety of reading related skills such as formulating deductions, finding ambiguous words in sentences, and classification. The first part of the program has a strong emphasis on story grammar, which prepares students for later writing. This part presents daily writing activities, but they are modest, compared to those that occur in the second part of the program.

The second part of the program (lessons 66–110) has a much stronger focus on writing. Students learn how to write paragraphs that tell the main idea of what occurred in an illustration and also tell about details that support the main idea. This part of the program also teaches writing-related skills, such as grammar, parts of speech, punctuating sentences, and editing passages that have errors.

Schedule

The Grade 2 Language-Arts component is designed to be presented to the entire class. It is not to be scheduled during the daily reading period. Periods for the language-arts program require 40–45 minutes per day.

The language arts component should never take priority over the reading program. If you try to teach both the language component and the reading component in the same period, you will not complete the reading program during the first-grade year. Students will therefore be behind in reading during the following year.

The language arts program contains 110 lessons, which is fewer than the number of reading lessons (145). This means that if you start the language arts program on the same day that you start the reading program and if you teach 4 lessons a week, you'll complete both the reading and the Language Arts program around the same time.

For Whom

The Grade 2 language arts component is appropriate for all students who have completed the reading grade 1 language arts component and all students who are placed in grade 2 of the reading program.

Organization

Both parts of the program follow the organizational format of all DI programs.

Skills That Matter

All the skills taught in the program are important. Those skills are

a) assumed by later work in reading, writing, and content areas;
b) are typically not taught in any form; and
c) can be taught uniformly to students who qualify for entering Grade 2 Language Arts.

The topics and skills presented are those that relate to what students can do and what they will be reasonably required to do in the subsequent grades. The activities focus on laying a solid conceptual foundation for writing and analysis of language.

Skills Taught in Tracks

Skills are organized in **tracks.** A track is an ongoing development of a particular topic. Within each lesson, work from 3 to 5 tracks is presented. The teaching presentations are designed so it is possible to present the entire lesson in 45 minutes (although some lessons may run longer and some shorter, and more time may be needed for lower performers).

From lesson to lesson, the work on new skills develops a small step at a time so that students are not overwhelmed with new information. Students receive enough practice both to master skills and become facile with them. Students, therefore, learn quickly about learning new concepts and realize that what they are learning has utility because they will use it.

In traditional programs, the curriculum is called a spiral, which means that students work exclusively on a particular topic for a few lessons. Then a new topic (often unrelated to the preceding topic) is presented. *Reading Mastery Signature Edition Lanuage* does not follow this format for the following reasons:

a) During a period, it is not productive to work only on a single topic. If new information is being presented, it is very easy for students to become overwhelmed with the information. A more sensible procedure, and one that has been demonstrated to be superior in studies of learning and memory, is to distribute the practice so that, instead of working 40–45 minutes on a single topic, students work each day for possibly 8 minutes on each of five topics.

b) When full-period topics are presented, it becomes very difficult for the teacher to provide practice on the latest skills that have been taught. Unless the skills that have been taught are used and reviewed, student's performance will deteriorate, and the skills will have to be retaught when they again appear. A more sensible organization is to present work on skills continuously (not discontinuously), so that students work on a particular topic (such as deductions) for part of 20 or 30 lessons, not for 5 or 6 entire lessons at a time. In this context of continuous development of skills, review becomes automatic, and the need for reteaching is unlikely because students use the skills in almost every lesson.

c) When skills are not developed continuously, students must learn a lot of new concepts during a short period and are expected to become "automatic" in applying the new concepts and skills. For most students, adequate learning will not occur. A better method is to develop skills and concepts in small steps so that students are not required to learn as much new material at a time. In this way they receive a sufficient amount of practice to become facile or automatic in applying what they learn.

d) When skills are not developed continuously, students and teachers may develop very negative attitudes about mastery. Students often learn that they are not expected to "learn" the new material because it will go away in a few days. Teachers become frustrated because they often understand that students need much more practice, but they are unable to provide it and at the same time move through the program at a reasonable rate. Again, the continuous development of skills solves this problem because students learn very quickly that what is presented is used, in this lesson, the next lesson and in many subsequent lessons. When the practice is sufficient, students develop the mindset or expectation needed for learning

mastery because the skill is something they will need in the immediate future.

e) When lessons are not clearly related to "periods" of time, the teacher has no precise way to gauge the performance of the students or to judge how long to spend on a particular "lesson." A more reasonable procedure is to organize material into lessons, each requiring so much time to teach. The teacher then knows that the lesson has the potential of teaching students within a class period of 40–45 minutes.

OVERVIEW OF TRACKS FOR PART I

This section of the guide provides an overview of Part I, lessons 1–65. A more in-depth discussion of these tracks begins on page 26. The tracks are explained below:

a) **Story Grammar.** When students read, they are expected to get a sense of the story so they can anticipate what will happen and can relate events that occur to what they know about the characters or the situations presented. To prepare students for this type of understanding, the program expands on what students know about story grammar. (See page 64 for a complete list of the stories.)

b) **Sequencing.** Students are expected to work with a static illustration and to interpret it as an event that is related to events that preceded it and events that follow. Students do a lot of work with temporal sequencing of events by interpreting pictures.

c) **Classification.** The major thrust of classification is to use information to eliminate possibilities. Students play a lot of clue games where they use information provided through clues to identify the mystery character or the mystery sequence. Students also do manipulations in which they make classes larger or smaller by manipulating subclasses that are within the larger class.

d) **Following Instructions and Writing Instructions.** Activities are designed so that students follow precise directions. Many of the activities involve maps. Students follow directions that involve distance and direction: "Go four blocks north; turn to the west and go three blocks." Students also make up such directions to get to specified objects.

e) **Constructing Deductions and Drawing Conclusions.** Later work in math, science, social studies and reading assumes an understanding of deductions and how to draw a conclusion from properly presented facts. The program presents students with a model that makes drawing conclusions easy. The model also allows students to identify deductions that are formally incorrect.

f) **Clarity.** Students work with pronoun clarity. "The bugs were in the bushes. They were red." The passage could have two meanings. The bugs could be red or the bushes could be red. The program presents many clarity activities in which students learn to identify the "unclear" word in passages like the one above. Students also learn to translate the possible meanings into concrete images. For example, they color pictures to show the two meanings for the passage above. (One picture has bugs that are red; the other has bushes that are red.)

g) **Perspectives.** Much of what students do in Grade 2 Language Arts prompts different perspectives. Stories give students information about motives that permit them to predict what will happen to familiar characters. The work with maps and diagrams prompts students to view static diagrams as sources of information about events that are linked to each other. Activities involving relative size and relative direction give students practice at viewing things from different perspectives.

h) **Writing.** Students work largely with sentences. Many of the sentences they write are prompted by illustrations. Students work from a variety of writing assignments. They write parallel sentences based on an illustration, write about story characters, complete deductions, label the category for different objects, write letters, and alphabetize words.

OVERVIEW OF TRACKS FOR PART II

Part II of the grade 2 language arts program (lessons 66-–110) provides teaching in all the component skills the student needs to organize and write basic passages. Writing is taught as a process, but one that involves the integration of skills that are pretaught, with initial writing assignments that are relatively simple and require only basic sentences that students are able to write. Progressive changes in writing assignments incorporate new skills that are taught in the program.

Communication Details

The ability to communicate in writing involves a host of higher-order thinking skills. For the simplest writing assignment, the student names the character in a picture and tells the main thing the character did. This assignment implies that the student is able to discriminate between "reporting" and "not reporting," and between "the main thing the character did" and some ancillary action.

Reporting

Initial writing assignments require students to report. Students learn to discriminate between sentences that "report" and those that don't report. Students are presented with a picture and a series of statements, some of which report on what the picture shows and others that don't.

Lesson 66

A

Circle **reports** if a sentence reports on what the picture shows.
Circle **does not report** if the sentence does not report on what the picture shows.

1. The three men were brothers.	reports	does not report
2. Three men fished from a boat.	reports	does not report
3. The men were going to have fish for dinner.	reports	does not report
4. A big dog stood in the boat.	reports	does not report
5. All the men wore hats.	reports	does not report
6. One man held a net.	reports	does not report
7. One fishing pole bent down toward the water.	reports	does not report
8. A large fish was on the end of the line.	reports	does not report

B Circle the part of each sentence that names.

1. The old man went to the store.

2. The man and the boy went to the store.

3. The horse jumped over the fence.

Students report on what pictures show. Students are not permitted to "make up" scenarios about what happened. Students describe what the characters did. They do not tell what the characters were thinking or feeling, or why they did what they did.

The grade 2 language program restricts initial writing assignments to "reporting" for several reasons:

a) Students of varying abilities will tend to write the same set of sentences if they are required to report. However, if students are permitted to write whatever their imagination dictates, great variation will occur. Although some of the students will write clever passages, these passages don't serve as good models to the other students because they are the product of many skills that have not been taught to the other students. Also, the lines between acceptable and unacceptable passages will not be clear to many students because the passage they write may be quite different from those other students created. In this context, students find it difficult to figure out what's acceptable and what isn't. In summary, when the assignment is restricted to "reporting," the criteria for an acceptable passage are clear, the variability from student to student is reduced, and all students are able to succeed because the assignment does not involve skills that have not been taught in the program. The goal is not to teach a few students well, but to teach all of them well.

b) To write effectively, the student must learn to operate under various constraints. Not all writing follows the same form; not all addresses the same reader. Ultimately, students will have to learn to "check" their passages for a large number of criteria. Writing that is limited to reporting is a good constraint for beginners.

c) The tests of reporting are relatively simple. Basically, if students cannot find details of a picture that correspond to what they wrote, they haven't reported.

Clarity

The clarity activities of part I are extended to part II. Part 2 teaches students the basic rules about clarity. In addition to the sentence format of first naming someone and then telling the main thing the person did, students are introduced to activities that focus on the idea that what somebody writes may be perfectly clear to the writer but not to the reader.

a) Initial exercises in clarity present pictures and a group of sentences.

Write the words that tell what people did.

1. see   2. go   3. sit   4. wear   5. run

Read each sentence. Write the letter of each picture that shows what the sentence says.

1. Brett ate fruit.
2. A person ate fruit.
3. Sandra ate an apple.
4. A person ate a banana.

Students identify the pictures each sentence could tell about. One sentence tells about only one picture. That is the preferable sentence, and that is the basic game of clarity—to describe so that the reader is able to visualize the details that are described by the passage in a way that creates very little ambiguity.

b) Students work with passages that "tell about" a picture, but that use unclear words. When the words are unclear, the passage could tell about any number of pictures. For instance, students are presented with a picture that shows a young girl, dressed in a cowgirl outfit, carrying a wooden basket containing a large, striped snake.

The passage:

An animal fell out of a large, old tree. It landed on the soft ground. A person picked it up. The person put it in a container and took it home.

All the sentences have parts that are vague. Students identify the vague words and replace them with more precise descriptions.

c) Students work with passages that have unclear pronouns and apply the rule that, if they are writing about more than one male or more than one female, sentences that use the words he or she may be unclear. For example:

Ann and Kim were swimming. She wore a bathing cap.

Students refer to a picture in which the girls are labeled and correct the second sentence to make it clear.

Passage Organization

Students are introduced to different organization schemes. The simplest organization involves writing more than one sentence about a picture. The first sentence tells the main thing the person did. The following sentences provide details. These exercises **teach** main idea and supporting detail in the appropriate context—writing. The tasks are relatively easy because students have already been taught the skills needed to write "main idea" sentences for pictures. Students simply tell the main thing the person did. After students have worked on simple assignments, they are presented with pictures that show groups of individuals. For example, a picture may show a group of students cleaning a room. No two students are doing the same thing, but all are engaged in the "main" activity of cleaning the room. Students start with the statement about what the group did; then they write about the individuals and tell what each of them did.

Editing

Editing activities are presented throughout grade 2 language. Their purpose is to reinforce the various communication skills and mechanical skills taught in the program. They are coordinated with the students' writing assignments so that students are not required to apply a particular rule, procedure, or skill until they have edited passages for violations of the rule, procedure or skill. For example, students edit passages for pronoun clarity before they are held accountable for writing passages that have clear pronouns. Students do not write passages with direct quotes until they have edited sentences that are supposed to present direct quotes.

The editing activities are extended to the students' writing through checks for specific aspects of what the students wrote. The rationale for checks is that students should first write and then check their writing for various criteria. This process is easier for students if they understand the various criteria. Checks are a very important part of the teaching that students receive. The specific checks for a writing assignment appear in the student textbook. Here's an example:

Check 1
Does each sentence begin with a capital and end with a period?

Check 2
Does each sentence tell the main thing?

Check 3
Does each sentence tell what somebody or something **did?**

After students write their stories, they read them for each of the checks. By dealing with the checks one at a time, students receive practice in applying criteria one at a time. Later, as they become more proficient at editing for multiple criteria, they will become more facile both at reading for multiple checks and for writing quickly and doing some checking at the same time.

For students, editing their own work is a difficult process. That's why they first learn particular skills in isolation, then they edit someone else's writing for violations, and finally they edit their own writing for possible violations.

Teaching the Program

Classroom Organization

Arrange seating so you can receive very quick information on high performers and low performers. A good plan is to organize the students something like this:

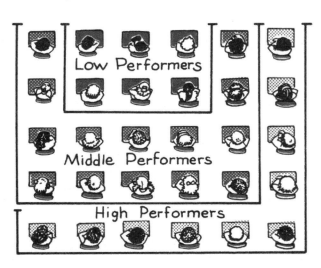

The lowest performers are closest to the front of the classroom. Middle performers are arranged around the lowest performers. Highest performers are arranged around the periphery. With this arrangement, you can position yourself so that, by taking a few steps during the time that students are working problems, you can sample low, average and high performers. While different variations of this arrangement are possible, be careful not to seat low performers far from the front-center of the room. The highest performers, understandably, can be farthest from the center because they attend better, learn faster, and need less observation and feedback. For some activities, students will work in groups or teams. The size of the groups varies. When assigning groups, make sure that each group has a range of students. (Don't put all the higher performers in one group.)

Teaching and Monitoring

When you teach the program, a basic rule is that you shouldn't present from the front of the room unless you're showing something on the board.

For most of the activities, you direct students to work specified tasks. For these activities, you should present from somewhere in the middle of the room (in no set place); and as students work the task, you should move around and quickly observe a good sample of students. Although you won't be able to observe every student working every task, you can observe at least half a dozen students in possibly 15 seconds. Rehearse the lesson before presenting it to the class. Don't simply read the text—act it out. Watch your wording. If you rehearse each of the early lessons before presenting it, you'll soon learn how to present efficiently from the script. In later lessons, you should scan the list of skills at the beginning of each lesson. New skills are in boldface type. If a new skill is introduced in a lesson, rehearse it. Most activities in the lesson will not be new, but will be a variation of what you've presented earlier, so you may not need to rehearse these activities.

Using the Teacher Presentation Scripts

The script for each lesson indicates precisely how to present each structured activity. The script shows what you say, what you do and what the student's responses should be.

What you say appears in blue type:

You say this.

What you do appears in parentheses:

(You do this.)

The responses of the students are in italics:

Students say this.

Follow the specified wording in the script. While wording variations from the specified script are not always dangerous, you will be assured of communicating clearly with the students if you follow the script exactly. The reason is that the wording is controlled, and the tasks are arranged so they provide succint wording and focus clearly on important aspects of what the students are to do. Although you may at first feel uncomfortable "reading" from a script (and you may feel that the students will not pay attention), follow the scripts very closely; try to present them as if you were saying something important to the students. If you do, you'll find after awhile that working from a script is not difficult and that students indeed respond well to what you say.

A sample script appears below.

3. Everybody, touch picture 1. ✔
   Who's in that picture? (Signal.) *Roger.*
   • What did Roger do in this picture?
   (Call on a student. Idea: *Sat on a hat.*)
   • Here's the sentence that tells what Roger did: **Roger sat on a hat.**
   4. Everybody, say that sentence. (Signal.) ◄——— How you secure group responses. **1**
   Roger sat on a hat.
   • (Repeat step 4 until firm.) ◄——— What you firm **2**
   5. For each space on the arrow, you'll write the words that are in one of the boxes below the arrow:
   6. Touch the first space on the arrow for picture 1. ✔
   What will you write in that space? (Signal.)
   Roger.
   • Touch the middle space. ✔
   What will you write in that space? (Signal.)
   Sat on.
   • Touch the last space. ✔
   What will you write in that space? (Signal.)
   A hat.
   • (Repeat step 6 until firm.)
   7. Your turn: Write sentence 1. Remember to spell the words correctly. Start with a capital letter and end with a period. Raise your hand when you're finished. (Observe students and give feedback.)

- (Write on the board:)

  Roger sat on a hat.

What you write **3**

- Here's what you should have for sentence 1. Raise your hand if you got it right.

8. Touch picture 2. ✔
   Now you're going to make up a sentence for picture 2. That picture shows what another character did.
- Who's in the picture? (Signal.) *Sweetie.*
- Raise your hand if you can say the whole sentence about what Sweetie did in picture 2. Remember to use words from the boxes below the arrows.
  (Call on a student.) *Sweetie sat on a hat.*
- Yes, Sweetie sat on a hat.

9. Everybody, say that sentence. (Signal.) *Sweetie sat on a hat.*
- (Repeat step 9 until firm.)

10. Your turn: Write the sentence on the arrow for picture 2. Write the words **Sweetie, sat on, a hat.** Copy the words carefully. Start with a capital letter and end with a period. Raise your hand when you're finished.
    (Observe students and give feedback.)
    How you secure group responses

Pace your presentation **4**

11. Touch picture 3. ✔
    Uh-oh, it's hard to tell what's in that picture. In fact, maybe there's not even a hat in that picture. Maybe there's a cake, maybe somebody sat on that cake.
12. Your turn: Write sentence 3. Start with the name of somebody. Then tell what that character sat on. Don't write one of the sentences you've already written. Raise your hand when you're finished.
    (Observe students and give feedback.)

The arrows show the four different things you'll do that are not spelled out in the script.

- You'll make sure that group responses involve all the students.

- For some exercises, you'll write things on the board.

- You'll also "firm" critical parts of the exercises.

- And you'll use information based on what the students are doing to judge whether you'll proceed quickly or wait a few more seconds before moving on with the presentation.

Arrow 1: Group Responses

Some tasks call for an individual student to respond. Some tasks call for group responses. If students respond in unison, you receive good information about whether "most" of the students are performing correctly. The simplest way to signal students to respond together is to adopt a timing practice—just like the timing in a musical piece.

Step 4 presents a task that students respond to in unison:

> Everybody, say that sentence. (Signal.)
> *Roger sat on a hat.*

You can signal when students are to respond by nodding, clapping one time, snapping your fingers or tapping your foot. After initially establishing the timing for signals, you can signal through voice inflection only.

Students will not be able to respond together at the appropriate rate unless you follow these rules:

a) Talk first. Pause a standard length of time (possibly 1 second); then signal. Students are to respond on your signal—not after it or before it.

b) Model responses that are paced reasonably. Don't permit students to produce slow, drony responses. These are dangerous because they rob you of the information that can be derived from appropriate group responses. When students respond in a drony way, many of

them are copying responses of others. If students are required to respond at a reasonable speaking rate, all students must initiate responses; therefore, it's relatively easy to determine which students are not responding and which are saying the wrong thing.

Also, don't permit students to respond at a very fast rate or to "jump" your signal.

To correct mistakes, show students exactly what you want them to do:

- I'm good at saying it the right way. My turn to say that sentence. **Roger sat on a hat.** Wasn't that great? Let's see who can do it just that way.
  Everybody, say that sentence. (Signal.)
  Roger sat on a hat.
  Good saying it the right way.

(**Note:** Do **not** respond with the students unless you are trying to work with them on a difficult response. You present only what's in blue. You do not say the answers with the students, and you should not move your lips or give other spurious clues about what the answer is.)

Think of unison responses this way: If you use them correctly, they provide you with much diagnostic information. They suggest whether you should repeat a task (because the response was weak). They permit you to get information about which students may need more help. They are therefore important early in the program. After students have learned the game, the students will be able to respond on cue with no signal. That will happen, however, only if you always keep a constant time interval between the completion of what you say and your signal.

Arrow 2: Board Work

What you write is indicated in the display boxes of the script. In the sample exercise, you make an arrow with boxes and words.
Scanning the display boxes in the script shows both what you'll write and how you'll change displays.

Arrow 3: Firming

When students make mistakes, you correct them. A correction may occur during any part of the teacher presentation that calls for students to respond. Here are the rules for corrections:

- You correct a mistake as soon as you hear it.

- A mistake on oral responses is saying the wrong thing or not responding.

In step 4, students may not say anything or may not correctly say "Roger sat on a hat." You correct as soon as you hear the mistake. You do not wait until students finish responding before correcting.

To correct, say the correct response and then repeat the task they missed.

> Some students: *Roger was . . .*
> Teacher: Roger sat on a hat.
> Your turn: Say that sentence.

Sometimes, one step in the exercise involves a series of oral tasks. In step 6, students produce these responses:

6. Touch the first space on the arrow for picture 1. ✔
   What will you write in that space? (Signal.) *Roger.*
   - Touch the middle space. ✔
     What will you write in that space? (Signal.) *Sat on.*
   - Touch the last space. ✔
     What will you write in that space? (Signal.) *A hat.*
   - (Repeat step 6 until firm.)

After correcting any mistakes **within** this series of tasks, you would return to the beginning of step 6 and present the entire step.

The note **(Repeat step _____ until firm)** occurs when students must correctly produce a series of responses. When you "repeat until firm," you follow these steps:

1) Correct the mistake. (Tell the response and repeat the **task** that was missed.)
2) Return to the beginning of the specified step and present the entire step.

"Repeating until firm" provides information you need about the students. When the students made the mistake, you told the answer. Did they remember the answer? Would they now be able to perform the step correctly? The repeat-until-firm procedure provides you with answers to these questions. You present the context in which the mistake occurred and the students can show you through their responses whether or not the correction worked, whether or not they are **firm.**

The repeat-until-firm direction appears only on the most critical parts of new-teaching exercises. It usually focuses on knowledge that is very important for the work the students are to do. If you didn't firm the students in step 6 of the exercise, in step 7 you would find some students writing words in the wrong place or not doing anything. You would have to correct each student individually, telling each what to do. By repeating until firm, you potentially save time because you have made sure that students are firm in their understanding of where the words go.

As a general procedure, follow the repeat-until-firm directions. However, if you're quite sure that the mistake was a "glitch" and does not mean that the students lack understanding, don't follow the repeat-until-firm direction.

The specific responses for some tasks are not what some students might say. Expect variability in some group responses. Accept any reasonable wording.

If you want to hold students to the wording that is in the script (which is not necessary for tasks that can be reasonably answered in other ways), say something like, "That's right." Then say the response you want. "Everybody, say it that way."

As a rule, if more than one answer is possible for the task you presented and you know that the students's answers are reasonable, don't bother with a correction. Just move on to the next part of the teacher script.

Arrow 4: Pace Your Presentation

You should pace your verbal presentation at a normal speaking rate—as if you were telling somebody something important.

(**Note:** The presentation works much better and the inflections are far more appropriate if you pretend that you're talking to an **adult,** not a young student. Make your message sound important.)

The most typical mistake teachers make is going too slowly or talking as if to preschoolers.

The arrows for number 4 show two ways to pace your presentation for activities in which students write or draw or touch or find parts of their workbook page. The first is a note to **(Observe students and give feedback).** The second is a ✔ mark. That's a note to check what the students are doing.

A ✔ requires only a second or two. If you are positioned close to several "average performing" students, check whether they are performing. If they are, proceed with the presentation.

The **(Observe students and give feedback)** direction implies a more elaborate response. You sample more students and you give feedback, not only to individual students, but to the group. Here are the basic rules for what to do and not do when you observe and give feedback.

1) Make sure that you are not at the front of the class when you present the directions for tasks that involve observing students's performance. When you direct students to write the sentence about Sweetie, move to a place where you can quickly sample the performance of low, middle, and high performers.

2) As soon as students start to work, start observing. As you observe, make comments to the whole class. Focus these comments on students who are (a) following directions, (b) working quickly, (c) working accurately. "Wow, a couple of students are almost finished. I haven't seen one mistake so far."

3) When students raise their hand to indicate that they are finished, acknowledge them. (When you acknowledge that they are finished, they are to put their hand down.)

4) If you observe mistakes, do **not** provide a great deal of individual help. Point out any mistakes, but do not do the work for the students. Point to the problem and say, "I think you made a mistake here. Look at the word 'Sweetie' in the box and see how it is spelled." If students are not following instructions that you gave, tell them, "You're supposed to write the whole sentence. Listen very carefully to my instructions."

5) Do **not** wait for the slowest students to complete the activities before presenting the work check, during which students correct their work and fix up any mistakes. A good rule early in the program is to allow a **reasonable amount of time.** You can usually use the middle performers as a gauge for what is reasonable. As you observe that they are completing their work, announce, "Okay, you have about ten seconds more to finish up." At the end of that time, continue in the exercise.

6) Continue to circulate among the students and make sure that they fix up any mistakes you identify.

7) If you observe a serious problem that is not unique to only the lowest performers, tell the class, "Stop. We seem to have a serious problem." Repeat the part of the exercise that gives them information about what they are to do.
(**Note:** Do not provide "new teaching." Simply repeat the part of the exercise that gives them the information they need and reassign the work. "Let's see who can get it this time. . . .")

8) While students do their independent work (coloring their pictures), you may want to go over any parts of the lesson with the students who had trouble. At this time, you can show them what they did wrong. Keep your explanations simple. The more you talk, the more you'll probably confuse them. If there are serious problems, repeat the exercise that presented difficulties for the lower performers.

Summary

The four arrows indicate how you'll interact with the students, Where you say something that requires them to respond, they may make a mistake. You should anticipate that possibility and be ready to correct. Some steps in an exercise are more critical than others. If students are to do things that are either mechanically difficult or conceptually difficult, you want to "pre-correct" as many mistakes as possible. These parts of the format are usually flagged with a note to **(Repeat until firm)**. You want to make sure that the students are keeping up with your presentation and that they are attending to what you say. The parts of the exercise with ✔ marks and the **(Observe and give feedback)** are your key for judging whether the students are attending and performing.

You want to give them feedback. You let them know when they are performing well in following your directions and when they are making mistakes. For some types of feedback, you'll write on the board. You'll also write on the board to show them how things work.

When you practice exercises in the program, look at the places where you interact with the students. Those are places where mistakes may occur and where you may have to respond to what the students are doing.

Managing Part I Activities

Part I of grade 2 has activities that deal with constructing outcomes. Students make arrows, color things according to rules, measure, cut, and arrange. In most lessons, students use pencil and crayons. In some lessons, students also use scissors. Students often lack facility in working quickly and efficiently with this material.

Here are general management procedures for shaping their behavior.

1. Make sure that each student has the material needed for the lesson. One plan is to announce at the beginning of the lesson that it's time for the language lesson. Introduce the rule that you'll count to ten. All students who have their pencil and crayons on their desk and in place by the time you finish counting receive a good-work point (or sticker).
2. Establish the rule that students are not to play with their crayons or pencil until you tell them to use them. "Remember, don't play with your

material." The simplest way to shape their behavior is to praise students who are working "big." "Wow, we have a lot of big people in this room. Everybody has their pencil and crayons in place and nobody is playing with them. Nice job." If playing with material becomes a problem, award bonus points (or stickers) for not playing with the material.

3. When pencils or crayons are used for activities that precede the story, establish rules for what students are to do with their material when they complete the activity. "Remember, when you're finished, crayons back in the box. Pencils back in place." Again, praise students who follow these rules.
    "I can tell a lot of people are already finished because I see a lot of desks with the material in its place. Good work."
    After the structured lesson has been completed, students color the story picture and possibly other parts of the worksheet. This activity does not have to be scheduled as part of the lesson, but can be presented during "seat work" time.
4. Demonstrate procedures that require mechanical skills. Some students often have trouble writing or drawing arrows quickly. The simplest way to shape this behavior is to tell the student: "You want to see somebody who knows how to to a super job? Watch me." Quickly complete the job. "See if you can do that." Observe the student later and give feedback on improvements. "You're doing a lot better—those are good arrows." With repeated feedback (based on the idea that the student will not perform perfectly for a while, but will tend to improve), skills are shaped quickly.
5. In lessons that require cutting, make sure that students have scissors. In some lessons, students cut out elements and place them on a specified part of the page. The element to be cut out is always positioned at an outer edge of the page so that students are required to cut only three sides of the element, which is always in a dotted box.
6. Many lessons require students to "draw" elements or write letters or words in the picture. The simplest way to shape this type

of activity is to post student's material where all can see it. A good plan is to post samples of good work.

All students have their best work posted. The material remains on display for one week. When students do a particularly good job on a part, reward them by posting that worksheet. "That's a super job of coloring that picture and writing all the words. We're going to put this worksheet on display."

Shaping Student's Performance

The directions for presenting the teacher script provide you with information about how to hold the student's attention and how to pace your presentation so you're responsive to them and they are following your directions. Some of the lower performers may require "shaping" that goes beyond the details provided by the lesson script. Ideally, you should shape these students so they can keep up with the rest of the class when you present **at a reasonable pace.** If you key your presentation to the lower performers, nobody benefits. You actually punish the higher and middle performers and make the lessons boring for most of the students. Here are some general shaping suggestions that will help you accommodate all the students except those who do not have the skills necessary to begin the Grade 2 Language Arts program.

If students take a great deal of time writing, coloring, or drawing elements, use a timer to shape their performance. First, observe average performers and see how long it takes them to complete the tasks that are time consuming. Use that information for establishing a baseline. If average performers take 1 minute to write a sentence, set the criterion for 1 minute.

Tell students, "I'm setting the timer for 1 minute. So you'll have to work pretty fast. But work carefully. Raise your hand when you're finished."

As students raise their hand before the timer goes off, quickly check their work and make announcements, such as, "Wow, a lot of people are working fast and carefully."

When the timer goes off, say, "Everybody who finished, raise your hand. . . . Next time, we'll see

if we have even more students who can finish before the timer goes off." Either allow the students who didn't finish a little more time, or present the next activity to the class with the understanding that you'll work later with the students who didn't finish.

Although this procedure may seem harsh, it will very quickly shape the performance of students who are physically capable of performing.

When performance improves and virtually all students are completing the task on time, change the criterion. "I'm not going to set the timer for 1 minute. I'm going to make it harder and set it for 50 seconds. That's going to be really tough. Let's see who can do it."

Continue to change the criterion as students improve until they are performing at an acceptable rate.

If you follow these pacing procedures, your students will work faster and more accurately. They will also become facile at following your directions.

If you don't follow these rules, you may think that you are **helping** students, but you will actually be reinforcing them for behaviors that you are trying to change. If you wait far beyond a reasonable time period before presenting the work check, you punish the higher performers and the others who worked quickly and accurately. Soon, they will learn that there is no "payoff" for doing well—no praise, no recognition—but instead a long wait while you give attention to lower performers.

If you don't make announcements about students who are doing well and working quickly, the class will not understand what's expected. Students will probably not improve much.

If you provide extensive individual help on independent work, you will actually reinforce students for not listening to your directions, for being dependent on your help. Furthermore, this dependency becomes contagious. If you provide extensive individual "guidance," it doesn't take other students in the class long to discover that they don't have to listen to your directions, that they can raise their hand and receive help and that students who have the most serious problems receive the most teacher attention. These expectations are the opposite of the ones you want to induce. You want students to be self-reliant and to have a **reason** for learning and remembering what you say when you instruct them. The simplest reason is that they will use what they have just been shown and that those who remember will receive reinforcement.

If you provide wordy explanations and extensive reteaching to correct any problems you observe, you run the risk of further confusing the students. Their problem is that they didn't attend to or couldn't perform on some detail that you covered in your initial presentation. So tell them what they didn't attend to and repeat the activity (or the step) that gives them the information they need. This approach shows them how to process the information you already presented. A different demonstration or explanation, however, may not show them how to link what you said originally with the new demonstration. So go light on showing students another way.

Because Grade 2 of the language arts program is carefully designed, it is possible to teach all the students the desired behaviors of self-reliance, knowledge about how to follow instructions and the ability to work fast and accurately. If you follow the management rules outlined above, by the time the students have reached lesson 20, all students should be able to complete assigned work within a reasonable period of time, and all should have reasons to feel good about their ability to do the activities.

As they improve, you should tell them about it. "What's this? Everybody's finished with part A already? That's impressive. . . ."

That's what you want to happen. Follow the rules and it will happen.

Managing Part 2 Paragraph Writing Activities

The writing activity in each lesson (beginning with lesson 85) is presented after the work on specific skills. Most writing activity involves the following:

- an introduction
- writing
- oral reading of some passages
- checks for specific criteria

The last two steps of this process (reading passages and checking them) **account for possibly half of what students learn about writing.** Students learn from the good models that are read and from the mistakes in the models that are read. The oral reading of passages, therefore, is extremely important in shaping the students' understanding of how to apply what they have learned to specific writing assignments.

The checks that follow the oral reading are also very important because they provide students with practice in applying multiple criteria to their passages.

Effective management techniques for presenting writing assignments assure that students will learn from the models and will become facile at checking their own work. These techniques also reduce the amount of time you spend marking papers. Following writing assignments, you mark papers (which is a job that can become overwhelming because students write a lot).

As Students Write

Here are the basic rules to follow as students write:

1. Read passages as students are writing. If you become practiced at moving from student to student, you can read most of what students write as they are writing. A good technique is to make a line on the paper to mark what you've already read.
2. Refer to the criteria given in the instructions when commenting on what students have written. If students did not follow the directions, tell them which directions they didn't follow. "You were supposed to start each sentence by naming someone or something. I think some of your sentences have problems. Read over what you've written and see if you can fix it up."
3. Do not spend a lot of time with one student. There will be time for fix-ups later. Don't stand around as a student tries to find and correct the problem. Instead, observe other students and possibly return to the problem student later.

4. For passages that have problems, put a dot in the margin for each line that has a problem. When you read the passage later, you can scan the part you've already read to see if the mistake has been corrected.

5. Make frequent comments to the class. These comments should focus on what students are doing well and specific mistakes observed in several students' writing. "Wow, we have some good opening sentences that tell the main thing about the group"..."Watch how you punctuate the sentence that tells what Bob said."
    If students have had problems with a particular skill in the past and are doing well, make comments to the class. "You are doing a super job with sentences that begin with the part that tells when."

6. Do not wait for all students to complete their passage. Allow a reasonable amount of time (based on the performance of a slower but industrious student's performance) for students to complete the passage. Then tell students to stop writing. (It's a good idea to let them know a minute or two beforehand how much time they have left.) If you wait for all students to finish, students' writing rate will not improve greatly because there's no payoff for writing faster. If writing rate is a problem, reinforce students who improve and who complete assignments within a reasonable time period. Students who do not finish on time should finish the assignment at another time during the day. Although schedules often make it difficult to work with these students, you may be able to schedule a time during which other students are engaged in independent work, or it may be possible to assign higher-performing students to work with slower students during the make-up time.

7. Praise improvement. Make announcements to the class. Be sure to praise improvement of the low performers. They should understand that they are not failing to meet your expectations. "Well, you sure wrote a lot more today than you did last time. Good writing. Keep it up."

As Students Read Their Passages

Following the writing, you will call on a few students to read what they've written. They haven't checked their work yet, and the reading should be presented within this context. You will point out specific problems and engage the class in attending to mistakes as well as to aspects that are good.

Here are the general rules to follow:

1. Provide constant reminders to students about the context: "Remember, some of the passages may have problems, but we're reading them before they are checked over and fixed up. If we find mistakes, that's good, because the writer will know what has to be fixed up."

2. Call on a mix of higher- and lower-performing students. However, do not call on lower performers unless you know that what they've written has very few mistakes. (You've read the passage or most of it.)

3. Make sure that students attend to the passages that are read and identify specific problems. (You direct students to raise their hand if they hear a problem.) A good technique is to model the behavior that you want students to perform. When **you** hear a problem, raise your hand. You may provide some kind of reinforcement for students who identify problems correctly. "When I hear a problem, I'm going to raise my hand, but not right away. If at least ten hands are up before I raise my hand, I'll call on a student to tell about the problem. If the student is right, the whole class receives a bonus." (Set a goal for bonus points. After the class has earned so many bonus points, the students receive a special treat of some sort.)

4. Establish a general rule that students are not to make fun of another student's writing or become derogatory. "Remember, everybody makes mistakes. We're reading the stories so we can help each other fix up the mistakes. We won't make fun of you if you happen to make a mistake, and you will not make fun of somebody else who makes a mistake. At the end of the year, you'll all be able to look back

at the mistakes you made at first and wonder how you could have made them."

5. Do not let mistakes go by without comment. Students will not learn to apply the skills and criteria if they are apparently unimportant. Teachers sometimes feel that they don't want to emphasize the negative, and they therefore don't comment on mistakes. This procedure is ineffective. You will not help students learn if you demonstrate that they do not have to apply what is learned. If none of the students identifies a problem, raise your hand and you identify the problem.

6. Make appropriate positive comments about passages that have been read. But make sure that you base your judgment on whether the assignment **follows the directions that you provided.** Also praise improvement. "I'm impressed with what Josh wrote. It's a lot longer than the last story he wrote and nearly all the sentences were good. Keep it up, Josh."

7. Tell students how to correct any mistake, including mistakes that are not specifically associated with the directions. If the student writes, "He didn't have no apples," tell the student how to correct the sentence.

    "Here's how you could fix up that sentence. He didn't have **any** apples." If students use awkward prepositions or phrases, tell them a better way. For example, if a student writes, "A man in a long beard stood next to the car," say something like, "Here's a better way to say that: A man **with** a long beard stood next to the car." Follow the general rule that you should tell students how to correct any awkward parts of sentences.

8. Do not make a great fuss about passages that incorporate newly taught skills unless the directions call for such incorporation. For example, as students are learning to construct sentences that begin with the part of the predicate that tells when, some students may use these sentences in their passage. The same is true of direct quotes and the other skills that are taught. The best response is something like this: "Tim's passage had sentences that begin with the part that tells when. In a few lessons, you'll all be doing that. But if your sentences begin with the subject, your sentences are just fine."

9. Do not praise any sentences or passages that are in violation of the directions for the exercise. If what the student wrote is in violation of the directions, tell the student, "You made up an ending to the story about Tom and Linda, but that's not what the directions told you to do. You'll have a chance to write endings later in the program, but you have to follow the directions." If you don't hold students to the directions, it won't be long before students totally ignore directions. If some students write involved sentences of a type that has not been introduced, warn the other students. "Amy told what Bill said, but you don't know how to punctuate those sentences yet, so you shouldn't be writing them."

As Students Check Their Passages

The final activity involves the checks that appear in the writing assignment. The checks are not always the same, and there are never more than three checks. However, the checks become very general near the end of the program. Here are the checks from a later lesson:

Check 1. Did you tell what Ron did and said in the first picture?

Check 2. Did you tell about four or more important things that happened in the missing picture?

Check 3. Are all your sentences written correctly?

Students are directed to read their passage for each check.

Here are procedures for making the checks effective:

1. Establish a procedure for making the checks important. An effective plan is to tell the students that, after each check, you'll pick three papers to test for that check. For each paper that has been fixed up or that meets the criterion for the check, everybody in the

class earns 1 point. Write the number of points the class earns on the chalkboard. Repeat the procedure for each check, looking at three different papers and again writing the number of points on the chalkboard. If some of the students are low performers, you may want to check their papers only on criteria you know they will meet. It's important, however, to make your checking practices appear to be random, so that students do not know when their papers will be checked. To make the system even more potent, you may include a provision that, if the class earns 9 points (3 points for each check), you'll award 5 bonus points. The points can be used for a weekly treat of some sort. The treat should have a price tag of 7 points per lesson. If students have three writing periods per week, the price tag is 21 points.

2. As students check their work, circulate among them and look at their papers. If you observe a sentence that has not been corrected, give the student general information about the problem. Do not identify the sentence with the problem. Say something like, "The first part of your paragraph—where you tell about the first picture—has a problem. Read it for Check 2. See if you can find it and fix it up."

3. Do not hover over the student as he or she tries to find and correct the problem. Observe other students. Then possibly return to see whether the student has found the problem sentence.

4. Students who have not completed their paragraph should make a line in the margin to show how much they have written. They check what they have written. Later, after they complete the passage, they hand it in without the last part being checked.

Marking Papers

After students complete their checks, they hand in their papers. You mark them. If the checks and your observations are performed well, it's a lot easier to mark the papers. The line you marked indicates how much of each paper you've already checked. Any dots in the margin indicate sentences that had problems. By scanning first to see if problem sentences were corrected and then reading the remainder of the paper, you should be able to process each paper in less than a minute.

The comments you write on the paper should help students learn and reinforce good practices. Here are some procedures that work well:

1. Correct improper grammar by writing the correct words above the incorrect ones. **Note:** Use this procedure only with respect to grammatical constructions that are not taught in grade 2 language. For instance: She walked slow. Adverb usage is not taught in the grade 2 language arts program. Correct the word **slow** in pencil. She walked **slowly.**

2. Do not penalize students for **all** spelling mistakes. Words that appear in the vocabulary box for each assignment should be spelled correctly; however, a student's paper may have many "invented" spellings. A good rule is to hold the students accountable for any "spelling words" they should know and any words in the vocabulary box. You can write **S** or **Sp** above these words to indicate they are misspelled. If you wish to show the student the spelling of other words that are misspelled, write the word in pencil above the misspelled word. By writing it in pencil, you make it easy for the student to erase the misspelled word, fix up the word and erase the word you wrote.

3. Use a general code for indicating other mistakes. You can refer to the checks and indicate in the margin the lines that have problems. Write (1), (2) or (3) to indicate which check was violated (Check 1, Check 2 or Check 3). Do **not** mark the part of the sentence that has a problem.

4. Make comments on the paper. You may use letter grades or just comments. Try to focus on improvement even if a paper has serious problems.

   Much better. Watch run-ons.
   or
   Good checking for 1. Be careful on Check 2.

For good papers, write comments such as:

Super! or *Great job!*

5. Try to return students' papers before the next scheduled language lesson. Students are to fix up any mistakes before you begin the next lesson. They are to show you that they have fixed up the mistakes. A good practice is to tell the students to put their corrected papers on their desk at the beginning of the next language lesson. You can either check the fix-ups then, or you can do it as part of your observation when students write their passage for the current lesson.

Here is a copy of a student's paper when the student handed in the paper. Note the three dots on the paper. These dots indicate errors. The student fixed up one error before handing in the paper. Also note the line which indicates the last line the teacher had read during the lesson.

Here is a copy of the paper after the teacher marks it. Note the **Sp** written over the misspelled word. This word appeared in the vocabulary box.

The word **terrible** is written over **terabul** since this word neither appears in the vocabulary box nor was in an earlier spelling lesson. The (1) in the margin refers to Check 1 which dealt with capitals and periods. The (1) indicates that there is an error regarding capitals or periods on that line. The (2) in the margin refers to check 2 which dealt with writing what happened, not what is happening.

Shaping Better Writing

Sometimes students will write as little as possible. This tendency usually indicates that they are getting punished for writing more than the necessary minimum. (Students tend to write less if all spelling mistakes are marked and if they are held accountable for correctly punctuating sentence forms that have not been taught.)

Here are procedures for shaping better writing and a greater amount of writing:

1. Read selections to the class that are good examples of what you want students to do. Do not read passages that are flowery, that contain sentence types that have not yet been introduced, or that violate any of the checks. As a rule, select passages that contain more that the minimum number of sentences. Point that out as you read the selection. "This next selection has six sentences. Listen . . ."

   After reading a well-written selection, refer to any checks that gave **some of the students** problems. "Did you notice that Amy had three sentences that begin with the part that tells when? Listen again . . ."

   Try to read at least one passage written by a lower performer. Make sure, however, that it meets the checks and does not contain sentences that have serious grammatical problems. "Here's a paper written by Mark. It's a little short, but it does a very good job of meeting all the checks. Listen . . ."

2. Post papers of the week. A good plan is to have a bulletin board with two labels: **Super** and **Good.** Students select their best paper for the week and you post it under the appropriate heading. Tell students whose papers are posted under **Good** that if they keep working hard, they'll have papers that are super. When a student who has never been posted under **Super** moves up to this category, acknowledge the student's performance. "This is the first time we have one of Kimberly's papers in the **Super** class. But I'll bet it won't be the last. Good work, Kimberly."

Encourage students. Read the posted papers.

Summary

The procedures are designed to—

1. Provide students with practice in successfully using the process of writing—initial writing, checking, and rewriting according to specific checks.
2. Provide them with a mind-set that anticipates possible problems associated with the criteria that are used to judge their works.
3. Allow them to fix up papers before handing them in.
4. Provide them with motivation to write more and to write better.
5. allow them to succeed.

The procedures will also make your work easier. You'll spend less time reading papers, correcting them, and trying to shape writing behavior.

Follow the procedures.

Development of Tracks For Part I, Lessons 1–65

This section shows the development of the major tracks in Part I. Part I of the discussion that follows includes teaching notes, which address the most common problems teachers encounter. A scope and sequence chart for Part I appears on page 4.

CLASSIFICATION AND CLUES

The different classification activities involve using clues, grouping objects, identifying larger classes and smaller classes, and creating clues to unambiguously identify a particular character or member of a class.

The logic of classification is that some things are in a particular class and some things are not in that class. As the number of things that are in the class grows, the number of things not in the class shrinks. The opposite is also true. As the number of things in the class shrinks, the number of things not in that class grows.

Here's part of the activity from lesson 2.

EXERCISE 5 Classification

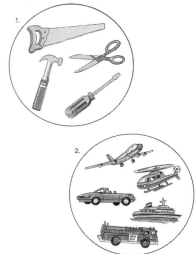

1. Everybody, find part D. ✔

- Touch circle 1. ✔
  The objects in circle 1 are **tools.** Listen: A tool is made to help you do work.
- Touch circle 2. ✔
  The objects in circle 2 are **vehicles.** Listen: A vehicle is made to take things places.
2. Everybody, what is a vehicle made to do? (Signal.) *Take things places.*
- What is a tool made to do? (Signal.) *Help you do work.*
- (Repeat step 2 until firm.)
3. Get ready to play a game. Listen carefully: I'm thinking of an object in one of the circles. I'm going to give you clues.
4. Here's the first clue: The object I'm thinking of is a **tool.** So you know which **circle** it must be in.
- Touch that circle. ✔
5. Here's the next clue: You use this tool to **cut.**
- Everybody, do you know which tool I'm thinking of yet? (Signal.) *No.*
- But you should know some tools I could not be thinking of.
  I could **not** be thinking of a hammer. Why not? (Call on a student. Idea: *You don't cut with a hammer.*)
- I could **not** be thinking of a screwdriver. Why not? (Call on a student. Idea: *You don't cut with a screwdriver.*)
- I **could** be thinking of the saw because it's a tool and you use a saw to cut. Or I **could** be thinking of scissors.
- How do you know I could be thinking of scissors? (Call on a student. Idea: *It's a tool and you use scissors to cut.*)
6. Here's the next clue: This kind of tool cuts wood.
- Everybody, do you know which tool I'm thinking of yet? (Signal.) *Yes.*
- Which tool? (Signal.) *The saw.*
- Listen: You cut with scissors. How do you know I wasn't thinking of scissors? (Call on a student. Idea: *They don't cut wood.*)

Teaching Notes

Always relate the correct answer to the clue that you give. For instance, you say, "You use this tool to cut." (Step 5) Then you ask the students to indicate why you could not be thinking of a hammer or a screwdriver. Often, students will "sort of" answer these items correctly. When asked how they know that you're not thinking of a hammer, they will say something like, "You pound nails with a hammer."

Do not accept such responses as correct. Say, "Listen: You use this tool to cut. Do you use a hammer to cut?" (Signal.) *"No."*
"That's why I could not be thinking of a hammer. Once more: Tell me why I could not be thinking of a hammer."
Use the specified students's responses to evaluate responses.

Starting in lesson 22, students learn subclasses of dogs. They learn to identify some hounds and some work dogs. By using a "class" box and a "not-class" box, students make different types of classes. Here's the activity from lesson 24. (**Note:** Students have already learned to identify and group some hounds and some work dogs.)

EXERCISE 2 Classification

Subclass: Dogs

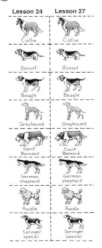

1. (Write on the board:)

Lesson 24

This says **Lesson 24.** Turn to the last page of your workbook and touch the column of dogs that has **Lesson 24** on top. Raise your hand when you've found it. (Observe students and give feedback.)

- You should be touching the column closest to the edge of the page.

2. Some of these dogs are work dogs, and some are hounds.
- Everybody, touch the first dog. ✔
  What dog is that? (Signal.) *Collie.*
- What group does a collie belong to? (Signal.) *Work dogs.*
- Touch the next dog. ✔
  What dog is that? (Signal.) *Basset.*
- What group does a basset belong to? (Signal.) *Hounds.*
- Touch the next dog. ✔
  What dog is that? (Signal.) *Beagle.*
- What group does a beagle belong to? (Signal.) *Hound.*
- Touch the next dog. ✔
  What dog is that? (Signal.) *Greyhound.*
- What group does a Greyhound belong to? (Signal.) *Hound.*
- Touch the next dog. ✔
  What dog is that? (Signal.) *St. Bernard.*
- What group does a St. Bernard belong to? (Signal.) *Work dogs.*
- Touch the next dog. ✔
  What dog is that? (Signal.) *German shepherd.*
- What group does a German shepherd belong to? (Signal.) *Work dogs.*

3. The rest of the pictures show dogs that aren't work dogs and aren't hounds.
- You're going to cut out that column. You'll start at the top and cut very carefully along the line. Cut carefully, because you're going to use this page in later lessons. Cut out the whole column of dogs. Raise your hand when you're finished. Now cut out each dog and we'll play a tough game. Raise your hand when you're finished.

CLASS AND NOT CLASS

1. Everybody, find part B. ✔

Class	Not Class

- Listen: One of the boxes has the word **Class** above it.
- Touch that box. ✔
- The other box has the words **Not-Class** above it.
- Touch that box. ✔

2. You're going to make up different classes. You make up a class by putting things in the class box. I'll tell you the name of the things for a big class.
- Listen: **Dogs.**
- Fix up your **class** box. Put all the dogs in the class box. Raise your hand when you're finished.
  (Observe students and give feedback.)
- You should have all the dogs in your **class** box. That's the biggest class you can make with your cutouts.

3. Now you'll make a smaller class by putting some dogs in the **not-class** box. Anything in the **not-class** box is **not** part of the class.
- Listen: Move all the cutouts that are **not** work dogs and **not** hounds to the **not-class** box. Leave all the hounds and work dogs in your **class** box. Raise your hand when you're finished.
  (Observe students and give feedback.)
- There should be two groups of dogs in the **class** box now. What are they?
  (Call on a student: Idea: *Hounds and work dogs.*)
- Yes, now the **class** box has hounds and work dogs.

4. Now you're going to make a smaller class.
- Listen: Put all your hounds in the **not-class** box. Don't move the other dogs out of the **class** box. Raise your hand when you're finished.
  (Observe students and give feedback.)
- There's a small class of dogs in the **class** box now. What's that class? (Signal.) *Work dogs.*

5. Now you're going to make a class that's even smaller.
- Listen: Move your St. Bernard and your collie to the **not-class** box. Now there's only one kind of dog in the **class** box. What's that? (Signal.) *German shepherd.*
- That's a smaller class than the class of work dogs.

6. Listen: Make the **biggest class** you can in the **class** box. Move dogs around so that you have as many dogs as possible in the **class** box. Raise your hand when you're finished.
  (Observe students and give feedback.)
- You have a very big class now. Everybody, what's the name of that class? (Signal.) *Dogs.*

7. Now see if you can move just some of the dogs to the **not-class** box so there are two large groups of dogs in the **class** box. Raise your hand when you're finished.
  (Observe students and give feedback.)
- What two large groups are in your class box now? (Signal.) *Work dogs and hounds.*
- What are the other dogs? (Signal.) *A poodle and a springer spaniel.*

8. Listen: Move one of the groups of dogs out of your **class** box and put it in the **not-class** box. Just one of the groups. You can pick either group you want to move. Raise your hand when you're finished.
  (Observe students and give feedback.)
- Now you should have a pretty small class.

9. Raise your hand if your **class** box has just hounds in it.
- Everybody with **hounds** in your **class** box, where are the work dogs? (Signal.) *In the not-class box.*
- Where are the other two dogs? (Signal.) *In the not-class box.*

10. Raise your hand if your **class** box has just work dogs in it.

- Everybody with **work dogs** in your **class** box, where are your hounds? (Signal.) *In the not-class box.*

- Where are the other two dogs? (Signal.) *In the not-class box.*

11. Listen: You're going to make the class so small that it has only one kind of dog in it. Move all the dogs but one of them to the **not-class** box. Raise your hand when you're finished.
(Observe students and give feedback.)

- You should have one dog in the **class** box and all the others in the **not-class** box. What does your **class** box show? (Call on individual students. Praise appropriate responses.)

- You're making up bigger and smaller classes. Good for you.

Teaching Notes

The activity shows the students the relationship between things that are in the class, things that are not in the class and all the things that you are considering. For this activity, the students are considering their cut-out dogs. For the biggest class, all cut-outs, are in the "class" box, and the class is dogs. To make a smaller class, some of the things from the "class" box move to the "not-class" box. The smallest class that can be made with the cut-outs is a single dog.

If students are firm on the relationship between the size of the class and the objects in the class, repeat steps 6 through 11. Tell students to listen carefully and work quickly. Praise students who follow your directions.

Beginning in lesson 32, students mentally manipulate the "class" and "not-class" box. Here's the first part of the exercise from lesson 32.

EXERCISE 3   Classification
Mental Manipulations

Class

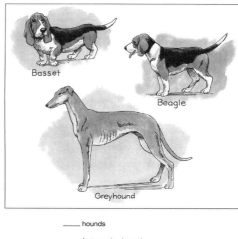

_____ hounds

_____ fast-running hounds

_____ dogs

_____ animals

1. Everybody, find part C. ✔
This picture shows a class. It doesn't show the not-class box.

- Listen: Raise your hand when you know the name of the smallest class shown in the class box. ✔

- Everybody, what's the class? (Signal.)

2. You're going to play the great thinking game. **Pretend** that you're going to change the class.

- Listen: You have hounds in the class box. But you want fast-running hounds in the class box. Just fast-running hounds. Think big. Raise your hand when you know whether you add things or take things out of the class box. ✔

3. Everybody, what do you do to the class box? (Signal.) *Take things out.*

- (Repeat step 3 until firm.)

4. Everybody, which class is smaller, **hounds** or **fast-running hounds?** (Signal.) *Fast-running hounds.*

- How do you know that the class of fast-running hounds is smaller? (Call on a student. Idea: *There are fewer things in the class of fast-running hounds.*)

- The class of fast-running hounds is smaller than the class of hounds. So you'll have to take things out of the class of hounds to get fast-running hounds.

- Listen: If you had the class of fast-running hounds in the class box, which dog would be in your class box? (Signal.) *The greyhound.*
- Where would the beagle and the basset be? (Signal.) *In the not-class box.*

5. New game: You have the class of hounds, but you want the class of **dogs.** Raise your hand when you know whether you'd add things or take things out.
- Everybody, what would you do to change the class box from hounds to dogs? (Signal.) *Add things.*
- Which class is bigger, hounds or dogs? (Signal.) *Dogs.*
- How do you know that the class of dogs is bigger? (Call on a student. Idea: *There are more things in the class of dogs.*)

Teaching Notes

If students incorrectly answer questions you present in steps 3 through 5, correct them by referring to the mental picture they should have of how to change the "class" box. For instance, in step 3 students do not respond firmly when you ask what you do to the "class" box (change it from the class of hounds to the class of fast-running hounds). "You have hounds, but you want fast-running hounds. Are all the things in the class box fast-running hounds?" (Signal.) *"No."*
"Where would the other things have to go?" (Signal.) *"To the not-class box."*
"So would your class box have more things or fewer things than it does now?" (Signal.) *"Fewer."*
Following mistakes on a "thinking game," repeat the game (steps 2–4 or step 5). Praise students for responding quickly and correctly.

Starting in lesson 35, students learn how additional information about a class member can reduce the membership of the class.
This activity is quite similar to the "mystery object" activities presented in Grade 1 and in Grade 2. (See Classification and Clues.)

EXERCISE 3 Classification

Mental Manipulation

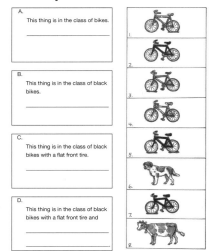

1. Everybody, find part C. ✔
   The pictures show different bikes. The sentences tell about the classes.
- I'll read the sentences. Follow along.
- Touch sentence A. ✔
  This thing is in the class of bikes. That's the big class.
- Touch sentence B. ✔
  This thing is the class of black bikes. That's a smaller class.
- Touch sentence C. ✔
  This thing is in the class of black bikes with a flat front tire.

2. Here's what you're going to do. Below each sentence, write the number of every picture that sentence tells about.
- Touch sentence A. ✔
  This thing is in the class of bikes. You have to write the number of every picture that sentence tells about. You'll write the number of every picture that shows a bike.
- Picture 1 shows a bike, so you'd write number 1 on the line below sentence A.
- Picture 2 shows a bike, so you'd write number 2 under the sentence.
- Listen: Write the number of every picture that shows a bike. Raise your hand when you're finished.
  (Observe students and give feedback.)
- (Write on the board:)

1, 2, 3, 4, 5, 7

- Here are the numbers you should have under sentence A—1, 2, 3, 4, 5, 7. Raise your hand if you got it right. ✔
- Everybody, look at picture number 6.
- Why didn't you write that number under the first sentence? (Call on individual students. Idea: *A St. Bernard is not a bike.*)
- Everybody, what other number didn't you write? (Signal.) *8.*
- Why didn't you write the number for Clarabelle? (Call on a student. Idea: *She's not a bike.*)

3. Touch sentence B. ✔
   This thing is in the class of **black** bikes. Is that class bigger or smaller than the class of bikes? (Signal.) *Smaller.*
- So you should have fewer things in this class.
- Write the number of everything that's in the class of **black** bikes. Raise your hand when you're finished.
  (Observe students and give feedback.)
- (Write on the board:)

   2, 5, 7

- Here are the numbers you should have for the things in the class of black bikes. Raise your hand if you got it right.

4. Touch sentence C. ✔
   This thing is in the class of black bikes with a flat front tire. Remember, it's in the class of **black** bikes with a flat front tire, not just any old bike with a flat front tire. Write the numbers for the things in that class. Raise your hand when you're finished.
   (Observe students and give feedback.)
- Everybody, which things are in the class of black bikes with a flat front tire? (Signal.) *5 and 7.*
- There are two things in that class, but we're going to tell about only one thing.
- Touch **only** bike 5. ✔
   That's the bike with the flat front tire you'll tell about.

5. Touch sentence D. ✔
   It says: This thing is in the class of black bikes with a flat front tire and . . . something else.

- You're going to complete that sentence so it tells about bike 5 and **no other** bike that's black and has a flat front tire.
- Look at the picture of bike 5. See what else you can say about that bike and write it. That bike has a flat front tire and something else. Raise your hand when you're finished. (Observe students and give feedback.)
- (Call on different students to read their sentence. Praise sentences that tell about a flat rear tire. Say:) That's a really super sentence: Raise your hand if you wrote that super sentence. (Praise sentences that tell about a flat rear tire.)
- This is pretty hard, but a lot of you are too smart to get fooled.

Starting in lesson 60, students write three sentences to identify a "mystery character." Each clue the students construct is designed to eliminate one or more possibility. Here's the activity from lesson 60.

WORKBOOK • LINED PAPER

EXERCISE 1 Test—**Writing Sentences**
Generating Clues

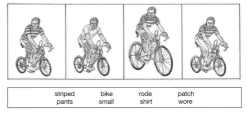

striped pants	bike small	rode shirt	patch wore

- This lesson is a test to see how smart you are. You can't talk to anybody during the test or look at what anybody else does.

1. Open your workbook to lesson 60 and find part A. ✔
   You're going to use lined paper and write clues that tell about the mystery man.

2. The mystery man is in the first picture.
- Touch that man. Make sure you're touching the right man or you'll make silly clues.
- All your clues should tell something that you can't say about all the men. Here's a bad clue: The man rode a bike. Why is that a bad clue? (Call on a student. Idea: *All the men rode a bike.*)

- Here's a good clue: The man had a patch on his pants. Why is that a good clue? (Call on a student. Idea: *Not all the men had a patch on their pants*.)
- Who can say another good clue? (Call on a student. Accept clues such as: *The man rode a small bike; The man wore a striped shirt*.)

3. (Write on the board:)

The man _____.

- You're going to write three clues. Somebody who reads all three clues would know exactly which man was the mystery man.
- Each clue will start with the words **the man.** Each clue will tell what the man wore or did.
- Touch the vocabulary box below the picture. I'll read the words: **striped . . . bike . . . rode . . . patch . . . pants . . . small . . . shirt . . . wore.**
- If you use any of those words, spell them correctly. Write your three clues. Remember the capital at the beginning and the period at the end of each sentence. Raise your hand when you're finished. (Observe students and give feedback.)

4. (Call on several students to read their set of clues. For each student, say:)
- Read your first clue. (Student reads.)
- Read your next clue. (Student reads.)
- Read your last clue. (Student reads.)
- (For each student, ask:)
  Everybody, do those three clues let you know which man is the mystery man? (Students respond.)
- (Praise good sets of clues.)
  Key: Good sets contain these 3 ideas in any order.
  The man rode a small bike.
  The man wore a striped shirt.
  The man had a patch on his pants.

Teaching Note

Earlier in the program, students learned about clues by working with sequences that showed a series of events over time. These sequences served to teach students the role of clues. (See Temporal Sequencing.) As a **group,** the clues should lead to the identification of only one character or one sequence. **Individually,** each good clue rules out one or more possibilities.

Temporal Sequencing

The activities on temporal sequencing are important for several reasons.

1. They present a picture sequence that corresponds to a sequence of events in time. When working with the sequence, students strengthen their understanding of this relationship.
2. The tasks present sentences that are temporally "backward." "Dud went tracking after he ate a ham bone." The first event that occurred in time was Dud eating a ham bone. However, this event is not named first in the sentence. Work with sentences of this type is important for the understanding of many things that are described in science and social studies.
3. The sequences lend themselves to many types of activities that involve "the mystery sequence." Grade 2 first introduces temporal sequences in lesson 27. Students work from a sequence of pictures that show which events occurred first, next and last. Students complete sentences that use the word "after."

EXERCISE 2　Temporal Sequencing

After

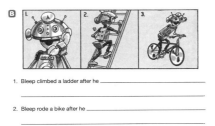

1. Bleep climbed a ladder after he _____
_____

2. Bleep rode a bike after he _____
_____

1. Find part B. ✔
   These pictures show what Bleep did first, next and last.
   - Touch the first picture.
     Everybody, what did Bleep do first? (Signal.) *Talked on the phone.*
   - Touch picture 2.
     That picture shows what Bleep did **after** he talked on the phone?
   - What did he do after he talked on the phone? (Signal.) *Climbed a ladder.*
   - Yes, Bleep climbed a ladder **after** he talked on the phone.
   - Touch picture 3.
     That picture shows what Bleep did after he climbed a ladder.
   - What did he do after he climbed a ladder? (Signal.) *Rode a bike.*
   - Yes, Bleep rode a bike after he climbed a ladder.
2. Touch the picture of Bleep riding a bike.
   Listen: Bleep rode a bike after he did something else. He rode a bike after he did what? (Signal.) *Climbed a ladder.*
3. I'll start with **Bleep rode a bike** and tell when he did that. Listen: Bleep rode a bike after he climbed a ladder.
   - Your turn: Start with **Bleep rode a bike** and tell when. Get ready. Go. (Signal.) *Bleep rode a bike after he climbed a ladder.*
   - (Repeat step 3 until firm.)
4. Touch the picture of Bleep climbing a ladder.
   Listen: Bleep climbed a ladder after he did something else. Bleep climbed a ladder after he did what? (Signal.) *Talked on the phone.*

5. I'll start with **Bleep climbed a ladder** and tell when he did that. Listen: Bleep climbed a ladder after he talked on the phone.
   - Your turn: Start with **Bleep climbed a ladder** and tell when. Get ready. Go. (Signal.) *Bleep climbed a ladder after he talked on the phone.*
   - (Repeat step 5 until firm.)
6. (Write on the board:)

   > **talked on the phone**
   > **climbed a ladder**
   > **rode a bike**

   - You're going to complete sentences. You'll have to pick the right part. I'll read each part: (Point to each part and read it.)
7. Touch sentence 1 below the pictures. It says: Bleep climbed a ladder after he . . .
   He climbed a ladder after he did something else. Write that something else. Raise your hand when you're finished. (Observe students and give feedback.)
8. Here's what you should have for sentence 1: Bleep climbed a ladder after he talked on the phone. Raise your hand if you got it right.
9. Touch sentence 2.
   It says: Bleep rode a bike after he . . .
   He rode a bike just after he did something else. Write that something else. Raise your hand when you're finished. (Observe students and give feedback.)
10. Here's what you should have for sentence 2: Bleep rode a bike after he climbed a ladder. Raise your hand if you got sentence 2 right.
    - Raise both your hands if you got both sentences right.
    - Those are very tricky sentences.

For sentence 1, students find the picture of Bleep climbing a ladder. They observe that Bleep climbed the ladder after he did something else. They describe that something else.

The next format presents students with a series of "arrows" that show different orders of events. The teacher gives clues about the mystery sequence. Students circle pictures for each clue. Each clue rules out one or more of the sequences. The first exercise appears in lesson 37.

EXERCISE 3 Clue Game

After

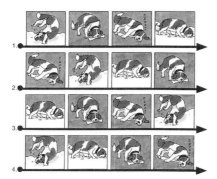

1. Everybody, find part B. ✔
   These four arrows show different things that Dud did.
- I'll give you clues. You'll figure out which arrows the clues tell about. To do that, you'll circle pictures I tell about.
2. Touch arrow 1. ✔
   The first picture shows Dud somersaulting in the snow. What did he do just after he somersaulted? (Signal.) *Ate a ham bone.*
- Yes, he ate a ham bone.
- What did he do just after he ate a ham bone? (Signal.) *Slept.*
- That last picture shows him tracking in the snow. That's what he did just after he slept.
3. Touch arrow 2.
   What did Dud do first? (Signal.) *Slept.*
- What did he do after he slept? (Signal.) *Somersaulted.*
- What did he do after he somersaulted in the snow? (Signal.) *Tracked.*
- What did he do after he tracked in the snow? (Signal.) *Ate a ham bone.*
4. I'm thinking about one of the arrows on this page. Here's the clue about the arrow I'm thinking of: On this arrow, Dud ate a ham bone just after he tracked in the snow.
- Find the first arrow that shows Dud ate a ham bone just **after** he tracked in the snow. Raise your hand when you know the first arrow with those pictures.

- Everybody, what's the number of the first arrow that shows Dud eating a ham bone just after he tracked in the snow? (Signal.) *Two.*
- (Draw on the board:)

- Look at the picture on the board. You're going to fix arrow 2 in your workbook so it looks like the arrow on the board. You draw one big circle around the pictures that show **Dud ate a ham bone just after he tracked in the snow.**
- Make your circle on arrow 2. Then find any other arrows that show **Dud ate a ham bone just after he tracked in the snow** and circle the pictures. Raise your hand when you're finished.
  (Observe students and give feedback.)
- Everybody, did you draw a circle around the pictures on arrow 3? (Signal.) *Yes.*
- Yes, the first two pictures on arrow 3 show Dud eating a ham bone just after he tracked in the snow. So you should have a circle around the first two pictures.
- Everybody, did you draw a circle around the pictures on arrow 4? (Signal.) *Yes.*
- Yes, the middle two pictures on arrow 4 show Dud eating a ham bone just after he tracked in the snow. So you should have a circle around the middle two pictures.
- Raise your hand if you have a circle on arrow 2, arrow 3 and arrow 4. ✔
- The mystery arrow could be any arrow that shows Dud eating a ham bone just after he tracked in the snow. One of the arrows could not be the mystery arrow. Raise your hand when you know which arrow could not be the mystery arrow. ✔
- Everybody, which arrow? (Signal.) *One.*
- Draw a line through the pictures on arrow 1 because it couldn't be the mystery arrow. Raise your hand when you're finished. ✔
5. Here's clue 2 about the mystery arrow: The mystery arrow shows Dud sleeping just after he ate a ham bone.

- Look at the arrows that are not crossed out. Draw a circle around the picture of **Dud sleeping just after he ate a ham bone.** Don't get fooled. Find him sleeping just after eating and circle him sleeping. Raise your hand when you're finished. (Observe students and give feedback.)
- You should have circled Dud sleeping on two arrows. What's the first arrow that shows Dud sleeping just after he ate a ham bone? (Signal.) *Three.*
- What's the other arrow that shows Dud sleeping just after he ate a ham bone? (Signal.) *Four.*
- You can cross out one more arrow because it doesn't show both clues about Dud. Raise your hand when you know the new arrow you can cross out. ✔
- Everybody, which arrow? (Signal.) *Two.*
- Draw a line through the pictures on arrow 2. It couldn't be the mystery arrow. It shows Dud eating a ham bone just after he tracked in the snow, but it doesn't show Dud sleeping just after he ate a ham bone.

6. Here's the last clue. Listen: The mystery arrow shows Dud somersaulting in the snow just after he slept. Listen again: The mystery arrow shows Dud somersaulting in the snow just after he slept.
- Circle any picture that shows Dud somersaulting just after he slept. Raise your hand when you're finished. (Observe students and give feedback.)
- You should have circled Dud somersaulting just after he slept on arrow 3.
- Now cross out any arrow that could not be the mystery arrow. Raise your hand when you're finished. ✔
- You should have crossed out arrow 4. Now you know the mystery arrow. It's the only arrow not crossed out. Everybody, which arrow is the mystery arrow? (Signal.) *Three.*
- Here's a tough question: Why couldn't arrow 4 be the mystery arrow? (Call on a student. Idea: *It doesn't show Dud somersaulting in the snow just after he slept.*)

7. Raise your hand if you followed all the clues and found the mystery arrow. Good for you.

Teaching Notes

Some students may make "reversals." For instance, in step 5, students may circle the pictures on arrow 2. To correct reversal problems, say the sentence. Then prompt the "after" relationship.

For example. "Listen: Dud was sleeping just after he ate a ham bone. He was sleeping just after he did something else. What did he do first? Find the right pictures."

The teacher script indicates that students should circle a single picture for clue 2 (step 5). Part of the reason for this specification is that students have trouble if their circles overlap (which is what happens on arrow 3 and arrow 4). The following is the workbook answer key for this exercise, showing how the student's workbooks should look.

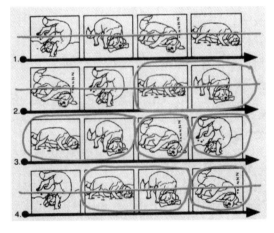

If students become confused, introduce a variation of the procedure in which students use different-colored crayons for circling different clues. For the first clue (step 4), students circle the **two pictures** with a red crayon. For the second clue, they circle **two pictures** with their blue crayon. They use a black crayon for their third clue. Below is the workbook answer key using different-colored crayons.

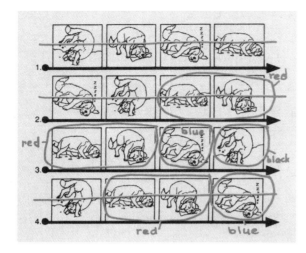

This activity is very sophisticated, but the students will do it if you take them through it a step at a time just as it is specified in the exercise. If students have trouble, post some of the better worksheets and praise the students who performed correctly.

A variation of temporal sequencing is introduced in lesson 51. For this variation, a single picture sequence is presented. Students complete two clues that tell about the sequence.

EXERCISE 2 Sentence Writing

Temporal Sequencing

1. _____

   after he played in the snow.
2. Dud _____

   _____ .

1. (Write on the board:)

> **Dud he after snow the ate went
> in ham bone played swimming**

- Find part B. ✔
  The pictures show Dud doing three things.
- Touch the first thing Dud did. ✔
  What did Dud do first? (Signal.) *Played in the snow.*
- Touch the next thing Dud did.
  What did Dud do after he played in the snow? (Signal.) *Ate a ham bone.*

- Touch the last thing Dud did.
  What did Dud do after he ate a ham bone? (Signal.) *Went swimming.*
2. You're going to complete sentences that tell what Dud did after he played in the snow and what he did after he ate a ham bone.
- (Point to the words on the board.) Here are some words you may use.
  (Touch each word as you say:) **Dud, he, after, snow, the, ate, went, in, ham bone, played, swimming.** If you use any of those words, make sure you spell them correctly.
3. Touch number 1. ✔
- On that line, you'll write what Dud did after he played in the snow.
- Touch the picture that shows what Dud did after he played in the snow. ✔
- Start your sentence with **Dud** and tell what he did after he played in the snow. Raise your hand when you're finished.
  (Observe students and give feedback.)
4. (Write on the board:)

> **Dud ate a ham bone after he played in the snow.**

- Here's what you should have for your first sentence: Dud ate a ham bone after he played in the snow. Raise your hand if you wrote everything correctly.
5. Touch number 2. ✔
- You'll write the whole sentence that tells what Dud did after he ate a ham bone.
- Touch the picture that shows what Dud did after he ate a ham bone. ✔
- The word **Dud** is already written. Tell what Dud did in the last picture. Then tell when he did it. Remember, Dud went swimming **after** he ate a ham bone. Raise your hand when you're finished.
  (Observe students and give feedback.)
6. (Write on the board:)

> **Dud went swimming after he ate a ham bone.**

- Here's what you should have for your second sentence.

- Raise your hand if you wrote everything correctly and if you put a period at the end of the sentence.

A later variation of the sentence-writing activity is presented in lessons 56 and 57. Students are presented with a group of sequences. They are assigned to write clues for one of the arrows. They write two clues. The first describes what occurred in the first two pictures. The next clue tells what happened in the second and third pictures.

Deductions

Deductions are important for work in science and social studies. Deductions are often assumed in everyday exchanges. Although students are familiar with the events and the logic, they are often unfamiliar with the verbal expression of the logic. For instance, they may have serious problems completing the last sentence in this item: "Everybody who works at the spa is in good shape. Debby works at the spa. So Debby . . . " To us, the last sentence is obvious: So Debby is in good shape. A very common response that students make, however, is: *"So Debby works at the spa."*

Grade 2 language presents deductions in a way that students learn very quickly how they work. The method involves putting the information on three arrows:

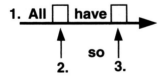

The top arrow presents the "rule." Arrows 2 and 3 apply the rule. These arrows tell about the two boxes on the top arrow. Arrow 2 gives information that something is in the class of things in the first box. Arrow 3 gives information that the same thing is in the class of things shown in the second box.

Exercises with deductions begin in lesson 8. Here's the introductory exercise.

EXERCISE 5 Deductions

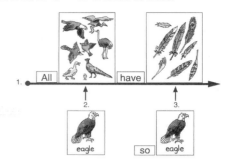

1. Everybody, find part D. ✔
    You're going to learn to say a 3-arrow deduction. This is tough, tough, tough.
2. (Draw on the board:)

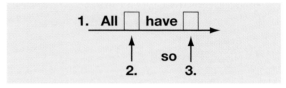

- (Touch arrow 1.) The first word on your arrows is **All.** Touch the word **All.** ✔
- Now touch the picture just after the word **All.**
- Everybody, what's in that picture? (Signal.) *Birds.*
- So the first part of the arrow rule is: **All birds.** What's the first part? (Signal.) *All birds.*
3. Touch the next word on arrow 1. ✔
    What's that word? (Signal.) *Have.*
- Yes, **have.**
- So the rule is: **All birds have . . .**
4. Touch the last picture. ✔
    The last picture shows what all birds have. What do all birds have? (Signal.) *Feathers.*
- **I'll** say the rule for arrow 1. **You** touch the things I say. Here we go: All . . . ✔
    birds . . . ✔
    have . . . ✔
    feathers. ✔
5. Everybody, say the rule for arrow 1. (Signal.) *All birds have feathers.*
- (Repeat step 5 until firm.)
6. Now touch the first arrow that goes **up.** That's arrow 2. ✔

- (Touch arrow 2.)

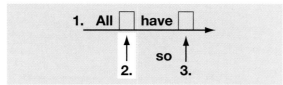

1. All ☐ have ☐
   ↑ 2. so ↑ 3.

- Here's the arrow you should be touching.
- There's a picture at the bottom of arrow 2. What's in that picture? (Signal.) *An eagle.*
- Arrow 2 shows that the eagle belongs in the first picture. **An eagle is a bird.** That's the rule for arrow 2: An eagle is a bird.

7. Everybody, say that rule. (Signal.) *An eagle is a bird.*
- (Repeat step 7 until firm.)
8. Touch the last arrow that goes **up.** That's arrow 3. ✔
- (Touch arrow 3.)

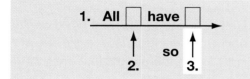

1. All ☐ have ☐
   ↑ 2. so ↑ 3.

- Here's the arrow you should be touching.
- What's at the bottom of that arrow? (Signal.) *An eagle.*
  Yes, it's an eagle again.
- The word next to that eagle is **so.** Touch the word **so.** ✔
  What's that word? (Signal.) *So.*
- Now go up arrow 3 and you'll see what the eagle has. What does the eagle have? (Signal.) *Feathers.*
- Here's the rule for arrow 3: **So an eagle has feathers.**
9. Say that rule. (Signal.) *So an eagle has feathers.*
- (Repeat step 9 until firm.)
10. I'm going to say the rule for all the arrows. I'll start with arrow 1.
- (Touch arrow 1 on the board.)
  Listen: **All birds have feathers.**
- (Touch arrow 2.)
  An eagle is a bird.
- (Touch arrow 3.)
  So an eagle has feathers.

12. Let's see if you can say the whole deduction. I'll tell you which arrow to touch. You say the statement for that arrow. Remember, you have to say the word **so** just before you say the statement for the last arrow.
13. Touch arrow 1. ✔
    Say the statement. (Signal.) *All birds have feathers.*
- Touch arrow 2. ✔
  Say the statement. (Signal.) *An eagle is a bird.*
- Touch arrow 3. ✔
  Say the statement. (Signal.) *So an eagle has feathers.*
- (Repeat step 13 until firm.)
14. See if you can say the whole thing. Remember, say the statement for arrow 1, then arrow 2, then arrow 3. Get ready. (Signal.) *All birds have feathers. An eagle is a bird. So an eagle has feathers.*
- (Repeat step 14 until firm.)
15. Raise your hand if you can say the whole deduction. (Call on a student. Praise correct response.)

Teaching Notes

Rehearse this format before you present it. If you know the steps and can deliver your lines fluently, the students will catch on quickly. Make sure you firm the different statements that students are to make. You are to firm in steps 5, 7, 9, 13 and 14.

Expect the first part of the exercise (through step 9) to move slowly. The last part (steps 10–15) should go fast. Make sure you hold students to a very high criterion of performance in steps 13 and 14. Position yourself where you can observe what students are pointing to and what they are saying.

Make a fuss over students who can say the whole deduction correctly (step 15).

If students are firm in this exercise, they will move through later exercises very quickly.

Variations of picture deductions are presented in lessons following lesson 8. A generically different type of deduction is introduced in lesson 25. Students construct a deduction to answer questions. This activity is similar to the one facing a story character, Sherlock, who is trying to solve a mystery and answer a question.

Here's the first part of the activity from lesson 25. In this exercise, students write deductions for three questions. Here's the part of the exercise that deals with the first question.

EXERCISE 3   Deduction Writing

1. Everybody, you're going to need these crayons: red and brown. Take them out. Raise your hand when you're ready. ✔
- Find part B. ✔
  This picture shows the afternoon, but not everything is shown in the picture.
2. Touch the toadstools. ✔
- Here's the rule about the toadstools: In the afternoon, all the toads are on toadstools.

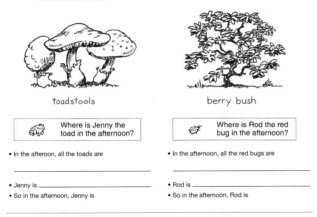

toadstools   berry bush

- In the afteroon, all the toads are   • In the afternoon, all the red bugs are

Where is Jenny the toad in the afternoon?   Where is Rod the red bug in the afternoon?

• Jenny is ___   • Rod is ___
• So in the afternoon, Jenny is   • So in the afternoon, Rod is

- Fix up your toadstools so they have brown toads on them. Raise your hand when you're finished.
  (Observe students and give feedback.)
3. Touch the box with the picture of the toad. ✔
  That's Jenny the toad.
- Touch the question in that box. ✔
- I'll read it: **Where is Jenny the toad in the afternoon?**

- Everybody, what does that question say? (Signal.) *Where is Jenny the toad in the afternoon?*
- You're going to tell about Jenny by completing the deduction below the box.
- Touch the first part of that deduction. ✔
  The first part says: In the afternoon, all the toads are . . .
- Where are all the toads? (Signal.) *On toadstools.*
- So the first sentence should say: In the afternoon, all the toads are **on toadstools.**
- Complete the first sentence. Raise your hand when you're finished. ✔
4. Touch the next sentence. ✔
  It says: Jenny is . . .
- What is Jenny? (Signal.) *A toad.*
- Finish that sentence. Raise your hand when you're finished. ✔
5. Now you can complete the last sentence. It says: So in the afternoon, Jenny is . . .
- Complete that sentence. Tell where Jenny is in the afternoon. Don't make the same kind of mistake the gray rat makes. Raise your hand when you're finished. ✔
- Here's what you should have for the last sentence: So in the afternoon, Jenny is on a toadstool. Raise your hand if you got it right. ✔
6. So you answered the question about Jenny. Where is Jenny in the afternoon? (Signal.) *On a toadstool.*
- And you wrote a deduction to tell how you figured it out.
- I can say the whole deduction: In the afternoon, all the toads are on toadstools. Jenny is a toad. So in the afternoon, Jenny is on a toadstool.
- Who thinks they can say that whole deduction without looking? (Call on several students. For each correct deduction, say:) You're sure a lot better at figuring things out than the gray rat is.

Teaching Notes

Although the wording for these deductions is slightly different from that presented earlier, students should have no trouble because the format of ordering the sentences is the same as that for earlier deductions.

In step 6, you call on different students to say the whole deduction about Jenny. If the students you call on tend to have trouble, say the whole deduction for the class and direct them to say the whole deduction together. Then call on several students to make sure that they are firm.

In lesson 39, students are introduced to deductions that are invalid because they do not present the three sentences in the appropriate order (1, 2, 3). Instead, they present them in this order: 1, 3, 2. The exercise in lesson 39 follows an episode of Sherlock in which he formulates invalid deductions.

EXERCISE 5 Deductions

1. (Draw on the board:)

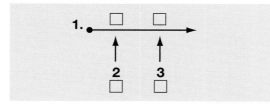

- I'll show you why Sherlock's deduction about who stole the corn doesn't work.
- For a good deduction, you do arrow 1, then arrow 2, then arrow 3. If you do the arrows in the wrong order, the deduction just doesn't work.
- Sherlock's deduction doesn't work because it does arrow 1, then arrow 3, then arrow 2.

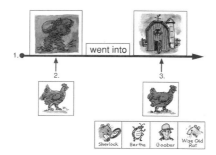

2. Everybody, find part D. ✔
   Touch arrow 1. ✔
   Here's the rule for that arrow: The corn thief went into the barn. Everybody, say that sentence. (Signal.) *The corn thief went into the barn.*
- Sherlock's first sentence says: The corn thief went into the barn. His next sentence should tell who the corn thief is. That's arrow 2. But he did arrow 3, not arrow 2. He told who went into the barn.
- Touch arrow 3. ✔
  Here's the statement for that arrow: The red chicken went into the barn.
- Touch arrow 2. ✔
  So the red chicken is the corn thief.
3. I'll say his whole deduction.
   Touch the arrows. ✔
- The corn thief went into the barn.
- The red chicken went into the barn.
- So the red chicken is the corn thief.
4. You say his whole deduction. I'll touch the arrows on the board.
- First sentence. (Touch arrow 1.) (Signal.) *The corn thief went into the barn.*
- Next sentence. (Touch arrow 3.) (Signal.) *The red chicken went into the barn.*
- Last sentence. (Touch arrow 2.) (Signal.) *So the red chicken is the corn thief.*
- That's wrong.
5. Below the arrows are some pictures of characters who went into the barn. Raise your hand if you can say the wrong deduction about Goober. (Call on a student. Touch arrows 1, 3, 2 on board as student says: *The corn thief went into the barn. Goober went into the barn. So Goober is the corn thief.*)
- Yes, that's not a good deduction.
- Raise your hand if you can say a wrong deduction about Sherlock. (Call on a student. Touch arrows on board as student says deduction.)
- Yes, that's a mixed-up deduction.
6. Sherlock's deduction is all mixed up. But listen to how silly it would sound if he put the sentences in the right order. I'll do arrows 1, 2 and 3 in the right order. Listen:

- (Touch arrow 1.) The corn thief went into the barn.
- (Touch arrow 2.) The red chicken is the corn thief.
- (Touch arrow 3.) So the red chicken went into the barn.
- No matter how you look at it, Sherlock is pretty mixed up.

Later in the program, students work with and construct deductions that are formally wrong.

Dialect

Starting in lesson 6 and continuing through lesson 59, students work on different *dialect* activities. The term *dialect* refers to speech that is transformed through a very specific change in the pronunciation of a particular sound. Regular talk can be transformed into dialect by changing the letters for the transformed sound in the dialect.

Different dialect exercises are presented. Each reinforces reading and pronunciation skills while it teaches a new sound game that students can extend to situations beyond the instructional context.

The first dialect exercise follows a story in which Bleep (a robot) adjusts his speaking mechanism so that he says the short **u** sound instead of the short **e** sound. Here's the exercise that follows the Bleep story in lesson 7.

EXERCISE 5 Correcting Bleep-Talk

1. Bleep said some strange things in this story. See if you know what he was trying to say.
- Listen: Bleep said, "I want to talk butter." Everybody, say that. (Signal.) *I want to talk butter.*
- Now say what Bleep was trying to say. (Signal.) *I want to talk better.*
2. Listen: Bleep said, "There is no stamp on this lutter." Everybody, say that. (Signal.) *There is no stamp on this lutter.*
- Now say what Bleep was trying to say. (Signal.) *There is no stamp on this letter.*

3. Listen: Bleep said, "I will gut a stamp." Everybody, say that. (Signal.) *I will gut a stamp.*
- Now say what Bleep was trying to say. (Signal.) *I will get a stamp.*
4. Here's a tough one. Listen: Bleep said, "Hullo, Bun." Everybody, say that. (Signal.) *Hullo, Bun.*
- Now say what Bleep was trying to say. (Signal.) *Hello, Ben.*
5. I'll say some other things Bleep might say. You tell me what he was trying to say.
- Listen: It's time to rust. Everybody, say it. (Signal.) *It's time to rust.*
- Now say what Bleep was trying to say. (Signal.) *It's time to rest.*
- Listen: Molly sleeps in a bud. Everybody, say it. (Signal.) *Molly sleeps in a bud.*
- Now say what Bleep was trying to say. (Signal.) *Molly sleeps in a bed.*

1. Everybody, find part C. ✔
   These are words that Bleep said.
   You're going to write the words Bleep was trying to say.
- Write the word **fed** below the word **fud.** Raise your hand when you're finished.
- (Write on the board:)

fed

- Check your work. Here's what you should have written below **fud.** Raise your hand if you got it right.

5. Touch word 4. ✔
- That word is **ugg.** What word was Bleep trying to say? (Signal.) *Egg.*
- Write the word **egg** below the word **ugg.** Raise your hand when you're finished.
- (Write on the board:)

> **egg**

- Check your work. Here's the word you should have written below **ugg.** Raise your hand if you got it right.
6. Raise your hand if you got all the words right. You're really good at figuring out what Bleep was trying to say.

In later exercises, students convert "regular" speech into "Bleep-talk." Different dialects are presented. One involves "non-nasal" talk. Here's an exercise from lesson 49.

EXERCISE 3 **Writing Non-nasal Speech**

1. Find part B. ✔
   This picture shows what would have happened if the big wind hadn't started blowing from the east at the end of the story.
- Molly is at the top of the basement stairs. See if you can read what she's saying.
- What is Molly saying? (Call on a student.) *Bleep, are you almost finished?*
- And Bleep is answering. Everybody, what is Bleep saying? (Signal.) *Yes.*
- That's what would have happened if the great wind hadn't started blowing.

- But when the wind started blowing, Molly had to wear something to protect her from the smell. What's that? (Signal.) *A clothespin.*
- And when she wore the clothespin, she couldn't say some of the words the right way. Raise your hand when you know which words she couldn't say.
- What's the first word she couldn't say? (Signal.) *Almost.*
- What's the next word she couldn't say? (Signal.) *Finished.*
2. Underline the word **almost** and the word **finished.** Then fix up those words so they say what Molly actually said with the clothespin on her nose. Cross out the letters she can't say. Write the letter she said above it.
- (Write on the board:)

> b   d
> al~~m~~ost fi~~n~~ished

- Here's what you should have.
3. Raise your hand if you remember what Bleep always said when he heard people talking in that strange way. Everybody, what did he say? (Signal.) *Blurp.*
4. Fix up Bleep so he says **blurp.**
- Cross out the word **yes** and write **blurp.** Raise your hand when you're finished.
- (Write on the board:)

> **Blurp**

- Here's what you should have.
- Later you can fix up that picture so it shows a clothespin on Molly's nose.

Directions (North, South, East, West)

The work on directions proceeds in three phases. First, students learn to face different directions in the classroom. Next, students learn the code for maps. (North is at the top; south at the bottom.) Finally, students engage in a variety of exercises that involve following instructions for getting to different places on a map or creating instructions. These instructions involve relative directions. (The place is north of something but south of something else.)

The concepts that are taught in the Directions track are important for students, both in terms of communication skills that are taught and in terms of the knowledge that makes future work in science and social studies easier and more comprehensible.

The work with directions begins in lesson 5 and continues through lesson 62. Here's part of the exercise from lesson 5.

5. I put the letters for directions on two walls.
- When I face **north,** I face the wall with **N** on it. Watch. (Face the **N** wall.) I'm facing north.
- Everybody, stand up.
6. Your turn: Face **north.** Get ready. Go. ✔ Which direction are you facing? (Signal.) *North.*
- Listen: When you face **north, south** is behind you.
- Everybody, face **south.** Get ready. Go. ✔ Which direction are you facing? (Signal.) *South.*
- (Repeat step 6 until firm.)
- Everybody, sit down.
7. I'll point to a wall. You tell me which direction I'm pointing.
- (Point **south.**) Everybody, which direction am I pointing? (Signal.) *South.*
- (Point **north.**) Which direction am I pointing? (Signal.) *North.*
8. Your turn: Everybody, point **south.** Get ready. Go. ✔
- Point **north.** Get ready. Go. ✔
- (Repeat step 8 until firm.)
9. Let's see who can do it without looking. Close your eyes. Keep them closed.
- Everybody, point **north.** Get ready. Go. ✔
- Point **south.** Get ready. Go. ✔
- Everybody, open your eyes and stand up.
10. (Remove **N** and **S** cards from the walls or corners.) This is tough.

- (Point to the **S** card.) Everybody, point to where the letter **S** goes. ✔
- What does the letter **S** stand for? (Signal.) *South.*
- (Point to the **N** card.) Point to where the letter **N** goes. ✔
- Everybody, what does the letter **N** stand for? (Signal.) *North.*
11. Wow, you are really getting smart about your directions.

Note: Save the **N** and **S** cards to post in lesson 6.

At the beginning of lesson 5 is a note to post **N** and **S** on appropriate walls or corners of the classroom. The format introduces only north and south. In lesson 8, east and west are introduced. All four directions are then reviewed in lessons 9 and 11. Here's the exercise from lesson 9.

EXERCISE 1   Directions

North, South, East, West

1. Let's see how well you remember the four directions.
2. Everybody, stand up and face **north.** ✔
- Face **south.** Get ready. Go. Everybody, face north again. ✔
3. Listen: Hold your **right** hand out to the side straight out. Get ready. Go.
- Everybody, which direction is your right hand pointing? (Signal.) *East.* Hands down.
- Everybody, hold your **left** hand out to the side—straight out. Get ready. Go.
- Think big. Which direction is your left hand pointing? (Signal.) *West.* Hands down.
- Which direction is **behind** you? (Signal.) *South.*
- (Repeat step 3 until firm.)
4. Everybody, face **east.** East. Get ready. Go.
- Which direction are you facing? (Signal.) *East.*
- When do you see the sun in the **east?** (Signal.) *In the morning.*

5. Everybody, face **west.** Get ready. Go.
- Which direction are you facing? (Signal.) *West.*
6. Everybody, face **north.** Get ready. Go.
- Get ready to **point** to different directions while you keep facing **north.**
7. Listen: Everybody, point to the **west.** West. Get ready. Go.
- Point **south.** South. Get ready. Go.
- Point **east.** East. Get ready. Go.
- Point **north.** North. Get ready. Go.
- (Repeat step 7 until firm.)
8. I can't fool you on the four directions. Sit down.

Teaching Notes

This sort of exercise should be fast and fun. All students should respond together and perform correctly. If you think that some students are "cluing" off others, direct them to close their eyes for some of the things they do. For instance, present step 3 having the students perform with their eyes closed. If students perform poorly in part of the exercise, repeat that part. Remember, the goal of these exercises is not merely to teach skills so that students are able to perform without a great deal of effort, but to teach the skills so they are relatively easy for students. Don't accept a sloppy performance from the students. Don't be afraid to repeat parts that are weak. Reinforce students who work quickly and accurately.

In lesson 12, students are introduced to the conventions for the directions on a map. Here's the first part of the exercise from lesson 12.

EXERCISE 2   Directions

Map

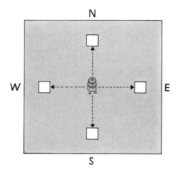

1. Open your workbook to lesson 12, and find part A. ✔
- This is a map. It has the letters **N, S, E** and **W** on it. Those letters stand for **north, south, east** and **west.**
2. Everybody, touch the letter **N.** ✔
   What does the **N** stand for? (Signal.) *North.*
- Listen: **North** is always at the **top** of the map.
- Everybody, touch the letter **S.** ✔
   What does the **S** stand for? (Signal.) *South.*
- Listen: **South** is always at the **bottom** of the map.
- Everybody, touch the letter **E.** ✔
   What does the **E** stand for? (Signal.) *East.*
- Everybody, touch the letter **W.** ✔
   What does the **W** stand for? (Signal.) *West.*
3. Everybody, pick up your workbook and stand up.
- Hold your workbook flat and face **north.** Make the arrow for **north** on the map point north in the room. ✔
- Now your map shows you just which way **east** and **west** and **south** are.

- Look at the arrow for **east** on your map. It points to your right. And that's just where **east** is in the room.
- Look at the arrow for **south.** It points right through you. And that's where **south** is, behind you.
- Remember when the **N** on the map points **north,** the arrows on the map show where all the other directions are.
- Everybody, sit down.
4. Touch the person in the middle of the map. ✔
   That person wants to walk **south.** Which direction does she want to walk? (Signal.) *South.*
- Look at the arrows that lead from the person. Write **S** in the box on the correct arrow. That arrow shows the direction she would go to walk **south.** Raise your hand when you're finished.
   (Observe students and give feedback.)
- (Write on the board:)

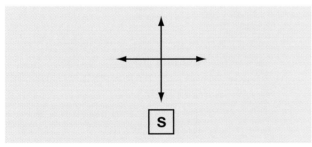

- Here's what you should have. Raise your hand if you got it right.
5. New problem: The person in the middle of the map wants to walk **east.** Which direction does she want to walk? (Signal.) *East.*
- Write **E** in the box on the arrow that shows which direction she would go. Raise your hand when you're finished.
   (Observe students and give feedback.)
- (Write to show:)

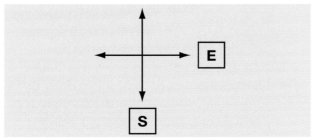

- Here's what you should have. Raise your hand if you got it right.
6. New problem: The person wants to walk **west.** Which direction does she want to walk? (Signal.) *West.*
- Write **W** in the box on the arrow that shows which direction she would go. Raise your hand when you're finished.
   (Observe students and give feedback.)
- (Write to show:)

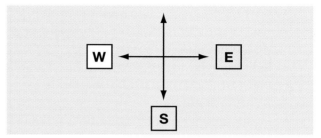

- Here's what you should have. Raise your hand if you got it right.

Teaching Notes

If the earlier work with directions in the classroom is done well, the students will have very little trouble understanding how the map works.

In step 3, students turn their map so that the directions on the map correspond to the directions in the room. This demonstration is important. It assures the students that you haven't introduced a new code for assigning the directions **north, south, east** and **west. Do not require students to turn their map to the north unless the exercise calls for this orientation.** If you always require this orientation, students will become greatly confused with later exercises.

In lesson 15, students use instructions about **north, south, east** and **west** to solve map puzzles. Here's the first part of the exercise.

EXERCISE 1   Directions

Map Puzzle

1. (Draw on the board:)

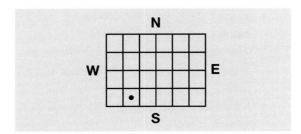

- You're going to work a puzzle. You'll have to move so many squares to the west or north or south or east.
- I'm going to move two squares to the east of the dot and put an **X** where I stop. Watch carefully.
- First I touch the dot. Then I count squares.
- **I DON'T START COUNTING UNTIL I START MOVING.**
- Listen again: I don't start counting until I start moving.
- Here I go. (Count:) One, two. (Make an **X** to show:)

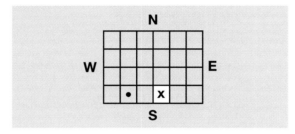

- I did it the right way.
2. Now I'll do it the wrong way. I'll say **one** when I touch the dot.
- Watch: (Touch the dot. Say:) One. (Move your finger 1 square east. Say:) Two.
- That's wrong because I started counting before I started moving.
3. Now I'm going to count three places **north** of the **X** I made.
- I touch the **X.** I don't start counting until I start moving.
- Here I go:
  One, two, three. (Move your finger up 3 squares north. Make an **X** to show:)

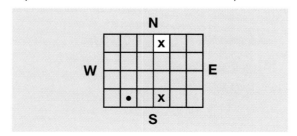

- I did it the right way.

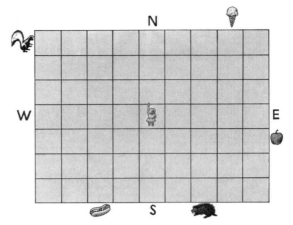

1. Open your workbook to lesson 15. ✔ Everybody, find part A. ✔
- This is a map puzzle. The girl in the picture will move to one of the things at the outside of the picture. The map has **N** at the top and **S** on the bottom. And it has **E** on one side and **W** on the other side.
2. Everybody, touch the girl in the picture. ✔
- She is pointing. Which direction is she pointing? (Signal.) *North.*
- Tell me which direction is to her **right.** Get ready. (Signal.) *East.*
- Tell me which direction is just **behind** her. Get ready. (Signal.) *South.*
- Tell me which direction is to her **left.** Get ready. (Signal.) *West.*
3. I'll tell you how the girl moves. You'll make a little **X** with your pencil to show where she ends up. If you do it right, you'll know whether she ends up at the skunk, the hot dog or one of the other pictures at the outside of the map.
- Listen: The girl walks **two** squares to the **east.** Remember, don't start counting until you start moving. Make a little tiny **X** in the square that is two squares to the east of where she starts out. After you make the little **X,** keep your pencil on that square because that's where the girl is now. (Observe students and give feedback.)
4. Listen: After the girl walks two squares to the east, she walks **one** square to the north. One square to the north. Make

- Open your eyes.
  Everybody, which direction does this arrow point **to?** (Signal.) *South.*
- Which direction does it point **from?** (Signal.) *North.*
- Yes, this arrow points **from** north **to** south.

Teaching Notes

In exercise 1, keep the pacing fast. Make sure students are performing accurately. If they are, they will have very few problems relating "to" and "from" to the map.

In lessons following lesson 23, students draw routes on maps to show story events. For example, following a story about Dot and Dud, students show the route the dogs took from the kennel north to the mountain.

In lesson 33, relative direction is introduced. The scheme involves asking how you get to an object. If you go north, the object is north. If you go south, the object is south. Here's the introductory exercise.

EXERCISE 2 **Map Directions**

Relative Direction

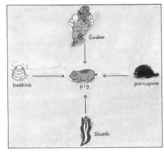

1. The pig is south of _____
2. The pig is north of _____
3. The pig is west of _____
4. The pig is east of _____

1. Find part B. ✔
- Here's one of those tough direction games again. The arrows show how to get to the pig from different places. Remember the rule. If you have to go north to get to the pig, the pig is north. If you have to go west to get to the pig, the pig is west.
- What direction is the pig if you have to go south to get to the pig? (Signal.) *South.*

- Right, it all depends on where you are.
2. If you were standing at the back end of one of those arrows, you'd have to go **north** to get to the pig. Find the arrow that points north.
- Write **N** on the point of that arrow. ✔
- Touch the object at the back end of the arrow. That's where you'd have to be standing to go **north** to get to the pig.
- (Draw on the board:)

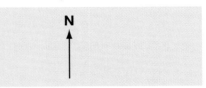

- Here's the arrow.
- (Touch the back end of the arrow.) Here's where you'd be standing.
- What object would you be standing on if you had to go north to get to the pig? (Signal.) *The skunk.*
- Phew. If you were standing on that skunk, you'd have to go north. So the pig is north of something. What's that? (Signal.) *The skunk.*
3. Say the whole thing about the pig. (Signal.) *The pig is north of the skunk.*
   - (Repeat step 3 until firm.)
4. If you were standing at the back end of one of these arrows, you'd have to go **east** to get to the pig. Find the arrow that points east.
- Write **E** on the point of that arrow. ✔
- Touch the object at the back end of that arrow. That's where you'd have to be standing to go east to get to the pig.
- (Draw on the board:)

- Here's the arrow.
- (Touch the back end.) Here's where you'd be standing.
- What object would you be standing on if you had to go east to get to the pig? (Signal.) *The beehive.*
- Ouch. If you were standing on that beehive, you'd have to go east to get to the pig. So the pig is east of something. What's that? (Signal.) *The beehive.*

- Ouch. If you were standing on that beehive, you'd have to go east to get to the pig. So the pig is east of something. What's that? (Signal.) *The beehive.*

5. Say the whole thing about the pig. (Signal.) *The pig is east of the beehive.*
- (Repeat step 5 until firm.)

6. If you were standing at the back end of one of those arrows, you'd have to go **south** to get to the pig. Write **S** on the point of that arrow. Figure out where you'd be standing to go south to get to the pig.
- (Draw on the board:)

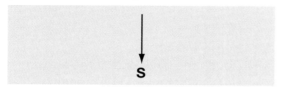

- Here's that arrow.
- (Touch the back end.) Here's where you'd be standing.
- What object would you be standing on if you had to go south to get to the pig? (Signal.) *Goober.*
- Phew. If you were standing where Goober is, you'd have to go south to get to the pig.

7. Say the whole thing about the pig. (Signal.) *The pig is south of Goober.*
- (Repeat step 7 until firm.)

8. If you were standing at the back of one of those arrows, you'd have to go **west** to get to the pig. Write **W** on the point of that arrow. Figure out where you'd be standing to go west to get to the pig.
- (Draw on the board:)

- Here's the arrow.
- (Touch the back end.) Here's where you'd be standing.
- What object would you be standing on? (Signal.) *The porcupine.*
- Ouch. What direction would you have to go to get to the pig? (Signal.) *West.*

9. Say the whole thing about the pig. (Signal.) *The pig is west of the porcupine.*
- (Repeat step 9 until firm.)

Teaching Notes

Rehearse this exercise before presenting it. If you understand the basic conventions for relating what you say about the object to how you get to the object, the teaching is not greatly difficult. Make sure, however, that students are very firm in saying the statements in steps 3, 5, 7 and 9.

In later lessons, students identify where characters are on a map based on assertions that the characters make about directions. Here's an activity from lesson 46.

EXERCISE 2   Map Directions

Relative Direction

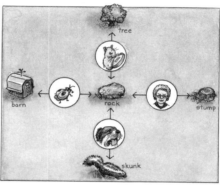

1. Bertha said, "The rock is _____ of me and the _____ is _____ of me."

2. Mrs. Hudson said, "The rock is _____ of me and the _____ is _____ of me."

3. Sherlock said, "The rock is _____ of me and the _____ is _____ of me."

1. Open your workbook to lesson 46 and find part A. ✔
   I'll tell you what different characters said. You're going to be a detective and figure out who could have said that.
- Here's what one character said: "The rock is west of me and the stump is east of me."
- Listen again: "The rock is west of me and the stump is east of me." Raise your hand when you know who said that.
- Everybody, who said, "The rock is west of me and the stump is east of me"? (Signal.) *Mrs. Hudson.*

- Yes, Mrs. Hudson.
- Here's what another character said: "The rock is north of me and the skunk is south of me."
- Listen again: "The rock is north of me and the skunk is south of me." Raise your hand when you know who said that.
- Everybody, who said, "The rock is north of me and the skunk is south of me"? (Signal.) *Dud.*
- Yes, Dud.
- Here's what the last character said: "The rock is east of me and the barn is west of me."
- Listen again: "The rock is east of me and the barn is west of me." Raise your hand when you know who said that.
- Everybody, who said, "The rock is east of me and the barn is west of me"? (Signal.) *Bertha.*

2. You're going to complete the items. They are tough. They all start by telling about the rock. But they have a lot of blanks.
- Touch item 1. ✔
  I'll read: Bertha said, "The rock is blank of me and the blank is blank of me."
- The first part of the sentence is: The rock is blank of me. Write the word for the direction. Raise your hand when you're finished. ✔
- The first part should say: Bertha said, "The rock is **east** of me."
- Then she says that something is in another direction. Name the object that is in the other direction and write the direction. Raise your hand when you're finished. ✔
- Here's what item 1 should say: Bertha said, "The rock is east of me and the **barn** is **west** of me." Raise your hand if you got it right.

3. Touch item 2. ✔
  I'll read: Mrs. Hudson said, "The rock is blank of me and the something else is blank of me."
- Complete the statement. Raise your hand when you're finished. ✔
- Here's what Mrs. Hudson said: "The rock is **west** of me and the **stump** is **east** of me." Raise your hand if you got it right.

4. Touch item 3. ✔
  Sherlock said, "The rock is blank of me and the something else is blank of me." Complete the statement. Raise your hand when you're finished. ✔
- Here's what Sherlock said: "The rock is **south** of me and the **tree** is **north** of me." Raise your hand if you got it right.
- Raise both hands if you got all those items right. I guess some of you are ready to be detectives.

Teaching Notes

This exercise presents two different skills. In the verbal exercise (step 1), students identify the character that could have made the assertion. In the writing exercise, students know who made each assertion. They fill in the blanks to complete the assertion.
To correct mistakes in the written work, tell the student who made a mistake:
1. "Touch the character."
2. "Tell how that character would move to get to the rock."
   "Go north."
3. "Say the fact about **the rock.**"
   "The rock is north of the character."
4. "Tell how that character would get to the other object on the arrow."
   (Student responds.)
5. "Say the fact about that object."
   "The _____ is _____ of the character."
6. "Write the correct description."

Following the introduction of relative direction, students work on different kinds of relative-direction exercises through the end of the program. Some of these exercises relate to later stories in the program (Dooly the Duck and Dessera).

Writing

In the first part of Grade 2 Language Arts, the students complete instructions for reaching different places on maps. They write statements that tell about relative direction. (The rock is east of me and the barn is west of me.) They write descriptions that tell about relative size. And they write sentences that tell about events that occurred after other events.

There are also on-going writing tracks. The writing activities in these tracks are designed to set the stage for future writing and to teach students about grammar and punctuation.

All sentence-construction activities present sentences that are of the form: subject-predicate. The reason is that sentences of this form are the most informative about both punctuation and grammar. More complicated sentences are often transformations of basic sentences. (A sentence such as, "After school, we went home," is a transformation of the subject-predicate sentence, "We went home after school.")

Writing Parallel Sentences

Beginning in lesson 1, students write simple parallel sentences. The picture shows two characters that are parallel in some way. You first direct students to copy the sentence that tells about one character. Then they write a parallel sentence that tells about the other character. Here's a sample exercise.

helpful	knock
jumpy	gate
farmer	landed
inside	

1. _____
2. _____
3. _____
4. _____
5. _____
6. _____
7. _____

The students copy the sentence about a rabbit. Then they write a parallel sentence about a turtle.

Constructing Sentences

In Grade 2, students learn the basic sentence-construction rule of naming and then telling more. In the initial exercises, they refer to a picture that shows a familiar character doing something. They name the character and tell what the character did. This procedure was introduced in Grade 1.

Here's an early sentence-construction activity from lesson 7 of Grade 2 language arts.

EXERCISE 3   Sentence Construction

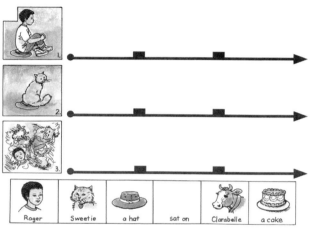

1. Everybody, find part B. ✔
   The pictures show what different characters did. You're going to write sentences that tell what the characters did in each picture.
2. Look at the boxes below the arrows. There are words at the bottom of each box. I'll read the words.
• Touch the first box.
   The word says: **Roger.**
• Touch the next box.
   The word says: **Sweetie.**
• Touch the next box.
   The words say: **a hat.**
• Touch the next box.
   There's no picture. The words say: **sat on.**
• Touch the next box.
   The word says: **Clarabelle.**
• Touch the last box.
   The words say: **a cake.**

3. Everybody, touch picture 1. ✔
   Who's in that picture? (Signal.) *Roger.*
 • What did Roger do in this picture? (Call on a student. Idea: *Sat on a hat.*)
 • Here's the sentence that tells what Roger did: **Roger sat on a hat.**
4. Everybody, say that sentence. (Signal.) *Roger sat on a hat.*
 • (Repeat step 4 until firm.)
5. For each space on the arrow, you'll write the words that are in one of the boxes below the arrows.
6. Touch the first space on the arrow for picture 1. ✔
   What will you write in that space? (Signal.) *Roger.*
 • Touch the middle space. ✔
   What will you write in that space? (Signal.) *Sat on.*
 • Touch the last space. ✔
   What will you write in that space? (Signal.) *A hat.*
 • (Repeat step 6 until firm.)
7. You turn: Write sentence 1.
   Remember to spell the words correctly. Start with a capital letter and end with a period. Raise your hand when you're finished.
   (Observe students and give feedback.)
 • (Write on the board:)

   Roger ■ sat on ■ a hat. →

 • Here's what you should have for sentence 1. Raise your hand if you got it right.
8. Touch picture 2. ✔
   Now you're going to make up a sentence for picture 2. That picture shows what another character did.
 • Who's in that picture? (Signal.) *Sweetie.*
 • Raise your hand if you can say the whole sentence about what Sweetie did in picture 2. Remember to use words from the boxes below the arrows. (Call on a student.) *Sweetie sat on a hat.*
 • Yes, Sweetie sat on a hat.

9. Everybody, say that sentence. (Signal.) *Sweetie sat on a hat.*
 • (Repeat step 9 until firm.)
10. Your turn: Write the sentence on the arrow for picture 2. Write the words **Sweetie, sat on, a hat.** Copy the words carefully. Start with a capital letter and end with a period. Raise your hand when you're finished. (Observe students and give feedback.)
11. Touch picture 3. ✔
    Uh-oh, it's hard to tell what's in that picture. In fact, maybe there's not even a hat in that picture. Maybe there's a cake, and maybe somebody sat on that cake.
12. Your turn: Write sentence 3. Start with the name of somebody. Then tell what that character sat on. Don't write one of the sentences you've already written. Raise your hand when you're finished. (Observe students and give feedback.)
13. Read the sentence you wrote for picture 3. (Call on several students. Praise sentences of the form _____ sat on _____.)
 • We have some pretty silly sentences.
14. Raise your hand if all your sentences start with a capital and end with a period.
 • Let's see who can read all three of their sentences. (Call on several students. Praise correct responses.)

Teaching Notes

The pictures form the basis for the sentences. In the early exercises, the pictures are carefully controlled so that students will succeed in their early writing endeavors. This feature is very important.
For picture 3, students make up a sentence. In step 13 of the exercise, you call on different students to read their sentences. Keep the pace moving or students may get into serious laughing fits.

In later lessons, students work on similar activities. In some, a picture is missing on the worksheet. Students write a sentence (usually a silly one) and later draw an illustration for the picture. These sentences and illustrations make good candidates for a lively bulletin board.

Composing Simple Stories

In lessons 21, 26 and 31, students compose simple stories based on a common theme or action. These stories follow a form of going from general to specific. The first sentence tells what everybody did. The following sentences tell what individual characters did. The pattern that is used is common in both poems and simple elaborations (main idea followed by detail).

The lessons in which these writing activities are presented differ from other lessons in Grade 2 language arts. The writing is the only activity presented in these lessons.

To compose their sentences, students refer to the illustrations and names on their workbook page. Here's the first part of the work in lesson 21.

WORKBOOK

Sentence Writing

Ⓐ

1. _____
_____
_____
2. _____
_____
_____
3. _____
_____
_____

1. Everybody, open your workbook to lesson 21 and find part A. ✔
• Today's lesson is different. You're going to write sentences. Then you're going to draw pictures for **two** of your favorite sentences.
2. Touch number 1. ✔
You're going to write your first sentence on the top line.

• (Write on the board:)

Everybody found something.

• This says: Everybody found something.
• Copy that sentence on the top line of number 1. Remember the capital and the period. Raise your hand when you've copied the sentence.
(Observe students and give feedback.)
3. On the next line you'll tell what **Goober** found. He found one of the things that you see at the bottom of the page. There are lots of things on that page. Maybe he found a puppy. Maybe he found that tub.
• Name something else he might have found. (Call on individual students.)
• (Write to show:)

Everybody found something.
Goober found _____.

• Here's the first part of the sentence. Write the sentence for Goober. Remember to spell the words just the way they are shown in the picture. Raise your hand when you've finished. Remember to start with a capital and end with a period.
(Observe students and give feedback.)
• (Call on individual students to read their sentence for Goober. Praise acceptable sentences.)
4. (Write to show:)

Everybody found something.
Goober found _____.
Liz _____.
I _____.

• On the next line you'll write what **Liz** found.
• On the bottom line you'll write what **you** found.
• Remember, each sentence starts with a capital and ends with a period. Raise your hand when you've written a sentence for Liz and a sentence for you.
(Observe students and give feedback.)
• (Call on individual students to read their sentence about Liz. Then call on individual students to read their sentence about themselves. Praise acceptable sentences.)

5. Touch number 2. ✔
   The sentences you'll write for number 2 tell what different characters **painted.**
   - (Write on the board:)

   > **Everybody painted something.**

   - This says: Everybody painted something.
   - Copy that sentence on the top line of number 2. Remember the capital and period. Raise your hand when you're finished.
   (Observe students and give feedback.)
6. (Write to show:)

   > **Everybody painted something.**
   > **Roger painted _____.**

   - On the next line you'll tell what **Roger** painted. He painted one of the things that you see at the bottom of the page. Maybe he painted a ladder. Maybe he painted a tub.
   - Write your sentence for Roger. Raise your hand when you're finished.
   (Observe students and give feedback.)
   - (Call on individual students to read their sentence for Roger. Praise acceptable sentences.)
7. (Write to show:)

   > **Everybody painted something.**
   > **Roger painted _____.**
   > **Molly _____.**
   > **I _____.**

   - On the next line you'll write what **Molly** painted.
   - On the bottom line you'll write what **you** painted.
   - Don't forget the capital and period for each sentence. Raise your hand when you've written a sentence for Molly and a sentence for you.
   (Observe students and give feedback.)
   - (Call on individual students to read their sentence about Molly. Then call on individual students to read their sentence about themselves. Praise acceptable sentences.)

Story-writing activities are also presented in lessons 34, 37, 43 and 46. The optional activities follow the same basic format as the exercise from lesson 21, except that students refer to their workbook page titled Story words. Here's the activity at the end of lesson 37.

EXERCISE 1   Sentence Writing

1. Everybody, find the page titled **Story words** at the front of your workbook.
   - Today, you're going to write sentences that make up little stories.
2. (Write on the board:)

   > **Everybody played.**

   - This says: Everybody played.
   - Copy that sentence on the second line of your paper. Remember the capital and the period. Raise your hand when you've copied the sentence.
   (Observe students and give feedback.)
3. (Write to show:)

   > **Everybody played.**
   > **Dot played with _____.**

   - Here's the first part of the sentence you'll write next. Dot played with blank. You're going to complete the sentence for Dot. She played with one of the things shown on the page with **Story words.**
   - Write your sentence about Dot. Raise your hand when you're finished.
   (Observe students and give feedback.)
   - (Call on individual students to read their sentence for Dot.)
4. (Write to show:)

   > **Everybody played.**
   > **Dot played with _____.**
   > **Zelda _____.**
   > **I _____.**

   - You're going to write more sentences. One will tell about Zelda and what she played with. The other will tell about you and what you played with.
   - Your turn: Write both sentences. Remember the period at the end of each

Reading Mastery **Grade 2**   Language Arts Teacher's Guide   **55**

sentence. Raise your hand when you're finished.
(Observe students and give feedback.)
- (Call on individual students to read their sentence about Zelda. Then call on individual students to read their sentence about themselves.)

Alphabetizing Skills

Starting with lesson 32, students alphabetize lists of words. Here's an example of the activity from lesson 32

ball	end
go	ant
dig	candy
fill	

1. _____
2. _____
3. _____
4. _____
5. _____
6. _____
7. _____

Letter Writing

Students also complete letters and a thank you note. Here is an example.

community center

The community center is east.	The community center is south.	The community center is west.	The community center is north.
Sherlock	Bertha	Zelda	Owen

Reporting

Starting in lesson 56, students learn about sentences that report. The rule is that a sentence reports on a picture if you can touch something in the picture that shows what the sentence says. Here's the exercise from lesson 57. Students indicate whether sentences report by circling the words **reports** or **does not report.**

WORKBOOK

EXERCISE 1   Reporting

1. Sherlock ate too much corn.	reports	does not report
2. Bertha was mad at Sherlock.	reports	does not report
3. Cyrus pulled a large sack.	reports	does not report
4. Bertha played a violin.	reports	does not report
5. The wise old rat was dirty.	reports	does not report
6. The sack was full of hazelnuts.	reports	does not report
7. The wise old rat was wet.	reports	does not report

1. Open your workbook to lesson 57 and find part A. ✔
   Look at the picture in part A. Remember, if a sentence tells about something that you can touch in the picture, the sentence **reports** on the picture. If the sentence does not tell about something you can touch, the sentence **does not report.**

2. Listen: Bertha played a violin.
   That sentence reports. Touch the part of the picture that shows: Bertha played a violin. ✔

   • Listen: Cyrus was mad at Sherlock. Everybody, does that sentence report? (Signal.) *No.*

   • Right, nothing in the picture shows: Cyrus was mad at Sherlock.

3. Listen: The sack that Cyrus was pulling belonged to Sherlock. Everybody, does that sentence report? (Signal.) *No.*

   • The picture doesn't show who the sack belongs to.

   • Listen: Two rats were sitting. Everybody, does that sentence report? (Signal.) *Yes.*

   • Touch the part of the picture that shows: Two rats were sitting. ✔

   • Listen: The wise old rat was taking a shower. Everybody, does that sentence report? (Signal.) *Yes.*

   • Listen: Bertha was playing a pretty tune. Everybody, does that sentence report? (Signal.) *No.*

   • It doesn't report because the picture doesn't show the music is a pretty tune. Maybe she's just making squeaking sounds.

4. Everybody, touch sentence 1 below the picture. Sentence 1.
   I'll read sentence 1: Sherlock ate too much corn. Everybody, does that sentence report? (Signal.) *No.*

   • The sentence does not report, so circle the words **does not report.** Find the words **does not report** on the same line as sentence 1 and circle them. ✔

5. Everybody, touch sentence 2.
   I'll read sentence 2: Bertha was mad at Sherlock. Everybody, does that sentence report? (Signal.) *No.*

   • The sentence does not report, so circle the words **does not report** on the same line as sentence 2.

6. I'll read the rest of the sentences. Touch each sentence as I read it. Don't circle anything. Just touch the sentences.

   • Sentence 3: Cyrus pulled a large sack.

   • Sentence 4: Bertha played a violin.

   • Sentence 5: The wise old rat was dirty.

   • Sentence 6: The sack was full of hazelnuts.

   • Sentence 7: The wise old rat was wet.

7. Your turn: Circle the right words for the sentences. Read each sentence to yourself. If the sentence reports, circle **reports.** If the sentence does not report, circle **does not report.** Raise your hand when you're finished.
   (Observe students and give feedback.)

8. Let's check your work. Look at the picture. Make an **X** next to any item you missed. I'll read each sentence. You tell me whether you circled **reports** or **does not report.**

   • Sentence 3: Cyrus pulled a large sack. What did you circle? (Signal.) *Reports.*

   • Sentence 4: Bertha played a violin. What did you circle? (Signal.) *Reports.*

   • Sentence 5: The wise old rat was dirty. What did you circle? (Signal.) *Does not report.*

   • Sentence 6: The sack was full of hazelnuts. What did you circle?
   (Signal.) *Does not report.*

   • Sentence 7: The wise old rat was wet. What did you circle? (Signal.) *Reports.*

9. Raise your hand if you got no items wrong. Great job.

   • Raise your hand if you got only 1 item wrong.
   Good work.

   • Listen: Fix up any mistakes you made in part A. Do it now. Circle the right words for any items you missed.
   (Observe students and give feedback.)

Teaching Note

When presenting steps 6, 7 and 8, circulate among the students. Allow students a reasonable amount of time to complete the work in step 7. In step 8, make sure they are correcting any mistakes.

Starting in lesson 57, students construct sentences that **report.** These sentences tell the main thing that a character did. Here's the activity from lesson 58.

WORKBOOK • LINED PAPER

EXERCISE 1   Sentence Writing

Reporting—Main Idea

1. Open your workbook to lesson 58 and find part A. ✔
   (Pass out lined paper.)
   • You're going to write sentences that report on the main thing that each character did in this picture. Each sentence you'll write will name the character and then tell what the character did.
2. Touch Bleep. ✔
   • Raise your hand when you know the main thing Bleep did.
   • Everybody, what did Bleep do? (Signal.) *Mopped the floor.*
   • Here's the whole sentence for Bleep: Bleep mopped the floor. Everybody, say that sentence. (Signal.) *Bleep mopped the floor.*
3. Touch Molly. ✔
   • Raise your hand when you can say the whole sentence that tells what Molly did. Remember, start with Molly and tell what she **did.**

   • (Call on a student.) Say the sentence for Molly. (Idea: *Molly washed the window.*)
   • Here's the sentence for Molly: Molly washed the window. Everybody, say that sentence. (Signal.) *Molly washed the window.*
4. Touch Paul. ✔
   • Raise your hand when you can say the whole sentence that tells what Paul did.
   • (Call on a student.) Say the sentence for Paul. (Idea: *Paul painted a piano.*)
   • Here's the sentence for Paul: Paul painted a piano. Everybody, say that sentence. (Signal.) *Paul painted a piano.*
5. Touch Zelda. ✔
   • Raise your hand when you can say the whole sentence that tells what Zelda did.
   • (Call on a student.) Say the sentence for Zelda. (Idea: *Zelda read a book.*)
   • I wonder if she's reading Mrs. Hudson's book.
   • Here's the sentence for Zelda: Zelda read a book. Everybody, say that sentence. (Signal.) *Zelda read a book.*
6. Touch the vocabulary box.
   That's the box with the words in it. These are words that you will use when you write your sentences. I'll read the words: **washed . . . mopped . . . read (red) . . . painted . . . book . . . window . . . floor . . . piano.**
7. Your turn: Write your sentence for Bleep. Start your sentence with Bleep. Tell what he did. Remember to spell the words correctly and end your sentence with a period. Raise your hand when you're finished.
   (Observe students and give feedback.)
   • (Write on the board:)

   Bleep mopped the floor.

   • Here's what you should have for your sentence that reports on Bleep.
8. Your next sentence will report on the main thing Molly did. Remember, start with Molly. Tell the main thing she did. Raise your hand when you're finished.
   (Observe students and give feedback.)

- (Write on the board:)

> **Molly washed the window.**

- Here's what you should have for Molly.
9. Your next sentence will report on the main thing Paul did. Start with Paul and tell the main thing he did. Raise your hand when you're finished.
   (Observe students and give feedback.)
- (Write on the board:)

> **Paul painted a piano.**

- Here's what you should have for Paul.
10. Your next sentence will report on the main thing Zelda did. Start with Zelda and tell the main thing she did. Raise your hand when you're finished.
    (Observe students and give feedback.)
- (Write on the board:)

> **Zelda read a book.**

- Here's what you should have for Zelda.
11. Raise your hand if you got all the sentences right. Good for you.
- Later you can color the picture. I wonder what color Paul painted the piano.

Clarity

Students entering the third grade often do not have a clear sense of pronoun referents. Their lack of understanding preempts them from comprehending much of what they read. They might read this passage, for instance: "The hunters rode their horses to the river. Their tails and manes blew in the wind." If you surveyed a sample of "average performing" third-graders, you'd discover possibly half of them think that the tails and manes belong to the hunters, not to the horses. These students will have serious comprehension problems when reading much of what they are expected to understand.

Understanding the use of pronouns is important also for writing clearly. Level B presents many exercises involving pronoun clarity, starting at lesson 34 and continuing to the end of the level.

The context for most of the exercises involves pictures.

Sentences are compared with pictures. For some activities, students change the sentences to make them clear. For other activities, students construct ambiguous sentences.

In lesson 34, students change the text that Mrs. Hudson wrote. The ambiguous word for each item is underlined. (The students replace the ambiguous word with the correct name.)

EXERCISE 5   Correcting Ambiguous Referents

1. My brother and my sister had pet pigs. They just loved to roll around in the mud.

2. We always kept a glass on top of the refrigerator. We kept it full of water.

1. Everybody, find part C. ✔
   Those are the sentences that Mrs. Hudson circled. The pictures show what she **wanted** Zelda's pictures to show. Mrs. Hudson could have changed the underlined part of each sentence so that Zelda would not have been mixed up.
2. Touch number 1. ✔
   I'll read what it says. Follow along:
- (Read slowly:) My brother and my sister had pet pigs. They just loved to roll around in the mud.
- Touch the word that's underlined. ✔
  Everybody, what word is underlined? (Signal.) *They.*
- Yes, **they. They** just loved to roll around in the mud.
- If Mrs. Hudson changed the word **they** to the right name, Zelda wouldn't have been confused. Everybody, what's the right name? (Signal.) *The pigs.*

- Listen: Cross out the word **they** and write **the pigs.** Raise your hand when you're finished.
  (Observe students and give feedback.)
- Now it says: My brother and my sister had pet pigs. **The pigs** just loved to roll around in the mud.
3. Touch number 2. ✔
   I'll read what it says. Follow along:
- (Read slowly:) We always kept a glass on top of the refrigerator. We kept it full of water.
- Touch the word that's underlined. ✔
  Everybody, what word is underlined? (Signal.) *It.*
- Yes, **it.** We kept **it** full of water.
- If Mrs. Hudson changed the word **it** to the right name, Zelda wouldn't have been confused. Everybody, what's the right name? (Signal.) *The glass.*
- Cross out the word **it** and write **the glass** above the crossed-out **it.** Raise your hand when you're finished.
  (Observe students and give feedback.)
- Now it says: We always kept a glass on top of the refrigerator. We kept **the glass** full of water. Now that's clear and Zelda would not be confused.
- Later you can color the pictures.

In lesson 35, students work with the same pair of items, but they indicate what Zelda (the confused artist) thought Mrs. Hudson wanted. (The students replace the ambiguous word with the unintended name.)

EXERCISE 5 Interpreting Ambiguous Sentences

1. My brother and my sister had pet pigs. <u>They</u> just loved to roll around in the mud.

2. We always kept a glass on top of the refrigerator. We kept <u>it</u> full of water.

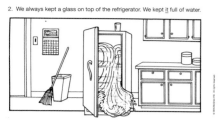

1. Everybody, find part D. ✔
   These are the illustrations that Zelda drew for two parts of the story.
- You're going to fix up the sentences with the names that Zelda thought the sentences were talking about.
2. Touch number 1. ✔
   The picture below number 1 shows Mrs. Hudson's brother and sister rolling around in the mud.
- I'll read what number 1 says. You follow along: My brother and my sister had pet pigs. They just loved to roll around in the mud.
- Touch the word that's underlined. ✔
  Everybody, what word is underlined? (Signal.) *They.*
- What was Mrs. Hudson **really** writing about? (Signal.) *The pigs.*
- What did Zelda think she was writing about? (Signal.) *Mrs. Hudson's brother and sister.*
3. Listen: Cross out the word **they** and write **my brother and sister** above the crossed-out word. Raise your hand when you're finished.
   (Observe students and give feedback.)
4. Touch number 2. ✔
   I'll read what it says: We always kept a glass on top of the refrigerator. We kept it full of water.
- Touch the word that's underlined. ✔
  Everybody, what word is underlined? (Signal.) *It.*
- What was Mrs. Hudson really writing about? (Signal.) *The glass.*
- What did Zelda think she was writing about? (Signal.) *The refrigerator.*

- Listen: Cross out the word **it** and write **the refrigerator.** Raise your hand when you're finished.
   (Observe students and give feedback.)

5. Now the sentences for both pictures tell what Zelda thought she should illustrate.
- Later you can color the pictures.

6. When you're done, you will have finished your first workbook. In the next lesson, you'll start a brand-new workbook.

There are three reasons for providing students with practice in making ambiguous sentences.

1. They find it to be a lot of fun.
2. It helps students understand the difference between the clear sentence and the ambiguous counterpart. The ambiguous sentence that students write as a "joke" is often the same sentence those students write when they are trying to be clear.
3. The work that students produce gives good evidence that they understand which words are potentially confusing.

In later lessons, students construct ambiguous sentence pairs that do not have prompted parts. For example, in lesson 47, students work with pairs of sentences. They identify the part of the second sentence that names something. They then use the appropriate pronouns to make the second sentence ambiguous. Here are the items.

C.

   1. The boys played with dogs. The dogs had short tails.
   2. The girls went in boats. The boats were made of wood.
   3. The truck went up a hill. The truck had a flat tire.

Here is the last part of the exercise. (Students have crossed out the first part of the second sentence in each item.)

5. (Write on the board:)

   He She It They

- To make the sentences confusing, you use one of these words. The words are **he, she, it, they.**
- You have to pick the right word to start the second sentence in each item.

- Touch item 1. ✔
   Everybody, what did you cross out in the second sentence? (Signal.) *The dogs.*
- You can use one of the words on the board to tell about the boys or the dogs. Raise your hand when you know which word that is.
- Everybody, which word? (Signal.) *They.*
- Yes, **they.** Write the word **they** above the crossed-out words.
   (Observe students and give feedback.)
- I'll read what item 1 should say now: The boys played with dogs. **They** had short tails.
- Now we don't know who had short tails. Maybe it was the dogs. Maybe it was . . . (pause) . . . **the boys.**

6. Item 2: The girls went in boats. The boats were made of wood.
- What did you cross out in the second sentence? (Signal.) *The boats.*
- You can use one of the words on the board to tell about the girls or the boats. Raise your hand when you know which word that is.
- Everybody, which word? (Signal.) *They.*
- Yes, **they.** Write the word **they** above the crossed-out words. Raise your hand when you're finished.
- I'll read what item 2 should say now: The girls went in boats. **They** were made of wood.
- Now we don't know what was made of wood. Maybe it was the boats. Maybe it was . . . (pause) . . . **the girls.**

7. Item 3: The truck went up a hill. The truck had a flat tire.
- What did you cross out in the second sentence? (Signal.) *The truck.*
- You can use one of the words on the board to tell about the truck or the hill. Raise your hand when you know which word that is.
- Everybody, which word? (Signal.) *It.*
- Yes, **it.** Write the word **it** above the crossed-out words. Raise your hand when you're finished.
- I'll read what item 3 should say now: The truck went up a hill. **It** had a flat tire.

- Now we don't know what had a flat tire. Maybe it was the truck. Maybe it was . . . (pause) . . . **the hill.**
8. There is a big box at the bottom of the page.
- Later you can draw a picture in that box to show how Zelda might illustrate one of those items.

Teaching Note

Make sure that students give strong verbal responses in steps 5 through 7. Often students are vague about the name that replaces "the dogs" or "the truck." If students give weak responses, go back to the beginning of step 5 and repeat the verbal work.

The focus of many clarity activities in Grade 2 Language Arts is on finding the ambiguity or the unintended meaning. The unintended meaning may be humorous. Students who do the various clarity activities in Grade 2 Language Arts learn this "game." It will help them greatly in both their future reading comprehension and in their writing.

Relative Size

Grade 2 Language Arts presents exercises involving relative size. The reason is that relative size assumes that one can take a particular viewpoint. A skyscraper is large when compared to us. The same building is tiny when compared to Pike's Peak.

Students learn about size perspective through a story involving Owen (a giant) and Fizz and Liz (people who are about one inch tall). Various relative-size exercises are generated from this story. For some activities, students view the world from the perspective of Owen. For others, they look at it as Fizz and Liz see it.

The work on relative size starts in lesson 12. Here's the first part of an exercise from lesson 19. Students describe things from the viewpoint of Fizz and Liz.

EXERCISE 4 Relative Size

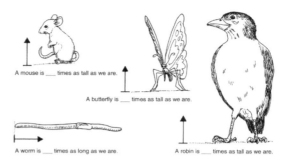

A mouse is ___ times as tall as we are.

A butterfly is ___ times as tall as we are.

A worm is ___ times as long as we are.

A robin is ___ times as tall as we are.

1. Everybody, find part C. ✔
   Along the bottom of the page is a pile of Fizzes and Lizzes.
- Cut out the whole strip. Cut along the dotted lines. Raise your hand when you're finished.
   (Observe students and give feedback.)
2. I'll read what it says under each animal.
- Everybody, touch the **mouse.** ✔
   It says: A mouse is blank times as tall as we are. It doesn't tell how many times.
- Touch the **butterfly.** ✔
   It says: A butterfly is blank times as tall as we are.
- Touch the **robin.** ✔
   It says: A robin is blank times as tall as we are.
- Touch the **worm.** ✔
   It says: A worm is blank times as long as we are.
- You're going to use your pile of Fizzes and Lizzes to figure out how they would describe the animals in the picture.
- You'll fill in the blanks with the right numbers.
3. Everybody, touch the **mouse** again. ✔
   Next to the mouse is a mark with an arrow going up from it. Put your pile of Fizzes and Lizzes on that mark and make the pile go in the same direction as the arrow. Put your pile so the **bottom** is right on the mark and the pile goes up. Raise your hand when your pile is in place.
   (Observe students and give feedback.)

4. Now you can start at the bottom of the pile and count the number of Fizzes and Lizzes to get to the very top of the mouse. Raise your hand when you know how many Fizzes and Lizzes it takes to get to the top of the mouse.
(Observe students and give feedback.)
- Everybody, how many Fizzes and Lizzes? (Signal.) *Two.*
- So that mouse is **two** times as tall as Fizz and Liz. Write **two** in the blank in the sentence below the mouse. Raise your hand when you're finished. ✔
5. Everybody, touch the **butterfly.** ✔
Put your pile so the bottom of the pile is on the line next to the butterfly. Then see how many Fizzes and Lizzes it takes to get to the very **top** of that butterfly's wing. Write the number for the butterfly, then write the number for the robin. Then stop. Don't do the worm. Raise your hand when you have numbers for the butterfly and the robin.
(Observe students and give feedback.)
- Everybody, touch the butterfly.
- Everybody, how many Fizzes and Lizzes is the butterfly? (Signal.) *Three.*
- Here's what your sentence should say: A butterfly is **three** times as tall as we are.

Teaching Notes

The problems that students encounter in exercises that require cutting and measuring are:
1. They work slowly and inaccurately.
2. They don't position their strips correctly (step 3).
To make the activity move, make sure that students have scissors before the exercise begins.
When students have finished cutting, they should put their scissors aside and hold up their strip to show they're finished. Praise students who finish quickly. If some students are working very slowly, present the rest of the activity to the students who are ready (starting with step 2).

In step 3, observe students carefully. The pile should be right side up. The bottom of the pile should be on the mark. Some students may have trouble identifying the top of the object they are measuring. If a student has trouble, tell the student, "Touch the very top of the mouse, then move your finger straight over to your strip. That's where you stop counting. That's the top of the mouse." If students follow the steps of positioning the strip, identifying the top of the object, and moving to the strip, they quickly catch on to how to measure. Without specific instruction, however, some of them remain quite confused.

Stories

In Part 1 of Grade 2 the central focus of each lesson is the story. The story typically comes at the end of the lesson. For the students, it's the payoff—the dessert. It is also the vehicle that both integrates what students learn and teaches them about the structure of stories. While it teaches "story grammar," the teaching focus is like that of the other activities in Grade 2—on construction. Students learn about stories in such a way that they can construct stories according to the constraints of different story grammars.

Part of each lesson presents a story or an activity that derives from one of the stories. All stories in part 1 of Grade 2 are designed to teach and expand on the concepts that are being taught to the students. Also, each major story has a unique story grammar that permits students to predict what will happen when a familiar character is engaged in a new adventure and permits them to create new stories based on the story grammar. Here's a list of the stories and the lesson in which each story is first presented. The stories in the first five lessons are stories that also appeared in the Grade 1 Language Arts program.

Lesson	Story
1	Paul Paints Plums
2	The Bragging Rats Race
3	Sweetie and the Birdbath
4	Clarabelle and the Bluebirds
5	Roger and the Headstand
6	Bleep Says Some Strange Things, Part 1
8	Paul Paints Pansies
11	The Mouse and the Toadstool
12	Bleep Says Some Strange Things, Part 2
15	Goober
16	Owen and the Little People, Part 1
17	Owen and the Little People, Part 2
18	Owen and the Little People, Part 3
19	Owen and the Little People, Part 4
22	Owen and the Little People, Part 5
23	Owen and the Little People, Part 6
25	The Bragging Rat Wants to Be a Detective
29	Dot and Dud, Part 1
32	Dot and Dud, Part 2
33	Dot and Dud, Part 3
34	Zelda the Artist, Part 1
35	Zelda the Artist, Part 2
36	Zelda the Artist, Part 3
38	The Case of the Missing Corn, Part 1
39	The Case of the Missing Corn, Part 2
41	The Case of the Missing Corn, Part 3
42	The Case of the Missing Corn, Part 4
48	Bleep Visits West Town, Part 1
49	Bleep Visits West Town, Part 2
51	The Case of the Squashed Squash, Part 1
52	The Case of the Squashed Squash, Part 2
53	The Case of the Squashed Squash, Part 3
55	Mrs. Hudson Writes Another Book, Part 1
56	Mrs. Hudson Writes Another Book, Part 2
57	More Silly Bleep-Talk
61	Zena and Zola, Part 1
62	Zena and Zola, Part 2
63	Dooly the Duck, Part 1
64	Dooly the Duck, Part 2
65	Dooly the Duck, Part 3
66	Dessera, Part 1
67	Dessera, Part 2
68	Dessera, Part 3
69	Dessera, Part 4

The stories at the beginning of Grade 2 (Paul, Sweetie, Clarabelle) were introduced in Grade 1. Here are summaries of the unique story grammars introduced in Grade 2.

Bleep and Molly

Bleep is a robot who talks and reasons. He sometimes removes the top of his head and fiddles with the screws that control the way he talks. He first adjusts two screws, causing him to be unable to say the short **e** sound. Instead, he says the short **u** sound. When trying to say "I will rest now," he says, "I will rust now."

In a later story, his creator, Molly, discovers that he is unable to say **s-l** combinations. He drops the **l** sound. Instead of saying "The stairs are slick," he says, "The stairs are sick."

In still another episode, Bleep adjusts his screws so that he talks like someone with a clothespin on his nose. He is unable to say the sounds for **m** and **n.** Instead of "win," he says, "wid." Instead of saying "mud," he says, "bud."

In a final episode, Bleep adjusts his speech so that he can't say the short **a** sound. Instead of saying "I am mad," he says, "I um mud."

The activities associated with Bleep stories capitalize on transforming dialect or correcting dialect. These activities both reinforce what students are learning about sounds and sound combinations and, at the same time, permit the students to play with codes that transform many utterances into "Bleep-talk."

Goober

Goober is a farmer whose story grammar is associated with sounds and smells. The sounds come from Goober's violin, which he plays beautifully. The smells come from Goober's pigs. Goober's pigs smell so bad that when people are around them, they hold their nose. Goober's problems end when a little girl from a nearby town brings him soap for pigs. Goober bathes his pigs and they no longer smell bad. Then the people can enjoy his beautiful violin music without being distracted.

Goober's adventures lead naturally to work with maps and directions. When the wind blows over his farm from west to east, his smell drifts to the town to the east of his farm. When the wind blows from east to west, the town to the west suffers. Goober's story grammar also leads to activities involving transformed speech and sound transformations. Students correct the speech of people who are holding their nose and saying things like "By dabe is Barry." (My name is Mary.)

Owen, Fizz and Liz

Owen and the Little People is a story about a giant (Owen) on one island and two very tiny characters (Fizz and Liz) on another identical island. Fizz and Liz are only about an inch tall. Owen has never seen Fizz and Liz, so he doesn't know how little they are. He communicates with them by sending notes in a bottle. He tries to describe his island. He tells how big things are by comparing the things to himself. On the other hand, Fizz and Liz don't know how big Owen is. They write answers by telling how different things are on their island. On Owen's island, there are very small bears. On the island of the little people, a bear's claw is bigger than a full-grown person.

Owen and his family decide to visit the island of Fizz and Liz. When they reach the island, they think that they must have made a mistake by returning to their own island. Finally, Owen locates Fizz and Liz and helps the little people with the construction of their community center.

The series about Owen and the little people presents many examples of perspective and relative size. It serves as a point of departure for measuring different things with "non-standard" units. For some workbook exercises, students use a "stack" of Fizzes and Lizzes to measure the height of objects. The height is expressed as "three times as tall as we are" or "five times as tall as we are." The series also reinforces concepts such as directions (north, south, east, west) and "continuous movement" (complicated routes that objects follow).

Sherloack and Bertha

Sherlock is one of the bragging rats from Grade 1. He decides to become a detective. One of his major problems is that he doesn't understand formal deductions or how to use clues to eliminate possibilities. Sherlock enlists the help of a beetle named Bertha to work with him. Bertha's role is to be that of a tracker. (She has a very good nose.) Although she is shy and initially reluctant to comment on Sherlock's plans, she has a good understanding of deductions and clues. She assists Sherlock first in the adventure of the missing corn. The rat pack's corn is stored in a barn and the supply is dwindling. Someone is stealing it. Sherlock makes this faulty deduction about the corn thief: The corn thief went into the barn; the red hen went into the barn; so the red hen is the corn thief. Sherlock tells the rat pack how he discovered the corn thief, and the rats start to use Sherlock's deduction to accuse each other. **"You** went into the barn, too. So you must have stolen the corn."

Bertha manages to straighten things out and later solves the crime. In another adventure, she and Sherlock use inferences to discover what happened to the squash that was being saved for the rat pack's annual fall feast.

The episodes with Bertha and Sherlock reinforce what students learn about deductions and clues. Some of the activities that accompany the stories present formally incorrect deductions, and the students have to identify their flaws. The series also lends itself to plays and to the creation of parallel adventures.

Dot and Dud

Another major series of stories is about two St. Bernards, Dot and Dud. They are siblings who work as rescue dogs in the mountains. Dot is diligent; Dud has the potential to be a great tracker, but he is lazy and playful. In their first episode, Dud gets separated from the ranger and the other dogs on a climb to find a stranded mountain climber. Dud becomes disoriented, goes in the wrong direction and ends up in the kitchen of a ski lodge miles to the south of the stranded climber. In the meantime, Dot finds the climber but is separated from the rescue party.

Near nightfall, the party abandons the search and returns to the ranger station for the night. Dud finds out that Dot is not with the other dogs. With determination, he tracks her that evening. The others follow him up the mountain, where they reach Dot and the stranded climber.

The Dot and Dud episodes reinforce what students have learned about "work dogs" (as part of classification exercises), about directions, maps, continuous movement, and how events may be correlated (the higher you go up the mountain, the colder the air gets).

Zelda and Mrs. Hudson

The Zelda and Mrs. Hudson stories teach students very sophisticated skills about clarity of expression. Zelda is a talented artist who is far better at illustrating than she is at interpreting unclear directions. Mrs. Hudson is the writer of a very boring book about her experiences. The book contains many unclear parts. Zelda agrees to do illustrations for Mrs. Hudson's book, and the results are humorous to the reader, but devastating to Mrs. Hudson.

To illustrate this part of the book—"My brother and my sister had pet pigs. They just loved to roll around in the mud."—Zelda draws a picture of the brother and sister rolling in the mud.

To illustrate this part of the book—"We always kept a glass on top of the refrigerator. We kept it full of water."—Zelda, with some difficulty, illustrates the refrigerator full of water.

Although Mrs. Hudson hates Zelda's illustrations, the book is a smash because of them.

The Zelda episodes serve as a point of departure for work on clarity. Typically, second graders do not understand unclear pronoun references. They quickly learn about clarity within the humorous context of Zelda's illustrations. The work on pronoun references (clarity) is expanded and becomes a major focus of Grade 2. Worksheet exercises require students to edit parts of Mrs. Hudson's story so the parts do not contain unclear pronouns, to draw illustrations for parts that have unclear pronouns and to construct passages that have unclear pronouns. This work, and the understanding that underlies it, is very

important for writing and for understanding exercises in later levels of the language portion of *Reading Mastery Signature* Edition.

In addition to alerting students to read a passage critically for possible ambiguity, the Zelda stories prompt students to imagine what the passage would say if the unintentional meaning were selected. Students indicate how Zelda would illustrate unclear passages.

Dooly and Duck

The sequence about Dooly the Duck focuses on a different spectrum of skills—following instructions, including those that involve relative direction (east of something but west of something else). Dooly is a Mallard duck who molts late one summer and cannot go with the other Mallards down the flyway to Mexico for the winter. He must remain in Minnesota while his feathers grow in. Then he will fly down to Mexico by himself.

Before the others leave, the head of the flock gives him directions about the first safe landing spot along the flyway. The landing place is between a hill and a walnut-shaped lake in Nebraska. The safe spot is "south of the hill and north of the lake." Dooly has a lot of trouble following these directions. After landing in the wrong place, he finally lands in the safe spot, where a crow teaches him more about following instructions that involve relative directions. Dooly learns fast and makes the trip to Mexico in record time. Later, he becomes the leader of the flock and successfully guides the flock on their annual migrations.

The Dooly stories reinforce what students have learned about relative direction and maps. The stories introduce the "flyway" that goes south from Minnesota to Mexico. Students learn the name of some states and become familiar with the map of North America—knowledge that will serve them well in later grades.

Dessera

The story about Dessera is the last sequence in Grade 2. Dessera is Queen of Garbo. She is young and headstrong. She visits the Rocky Mountains, where she plans to ski and climb

- Now underline the part of sentence 1 that tells more.
  (Observe students and give feedback.)
- Everybody, read the words you underlined. (Signal.) *Sat on a horse.*

4. Touch sentence 2.
   They rode the horse across the field. Say the part of the sentence that names. (Signal.) *They.*
- Say the part of the sentence that tells more. (Signal.) *Rode the horse across the field.*
- (Repeat step 4 until firm.)

5. Circle the part of the sentence that names and underline the part that tells more. (Observe students and give feedback.)
- Everybody, read the part of sentence 2 that names. (Signal.) *They.*
- Read the part that tells more. (Signal.) *Rode the horse across the field.*

6. I'll read the rest of the sentences in part C. Touch each sentence as I read it.
   Sentence 3: Their horse jumped over a fence.
   Sentence 4: A girl and her horse went across a stream.
   Sentence 5: She rested under a tree.
- For each sentence, circle the part of the sentence that names. Underline the part that tells more. Do it now. Raise your hand when you're finished.
  (Observe students and give feedback.)

7. Let's check your work. Make an **X** next to any item you missed.
- Sentence 3: Their horse jumped over a fence. Say that sentence. (Signal.) *Their horse jumped over a fence.* What part names? (Signal.) *Their horse.*
  What part tells more? (Signal.) *Jumped over a fence.*
- Sentence 4. A girl and her horse went across a stream. Say that sentence. (Signal.) *A girl and her horse went across a stream.* What part names? (Signal.) *A girl and her horse.*
  What part tells more? (Signal.) *Went across a stream.*

8. Raise your hand if you got no items wrong. Great job.

- Raise your hand if you got 1 item wrong. Good work.
- Fix up any mistakes you made in part C. (Observe students and give feedback.)

Teaching Notes

Students will have little trouble identifying the part that tells more if they are firm on identifying the part that names. The part that tells more is simply the rest of the sentence. You should present exercises like the one above at a rapid pace.

Beginning in lesson 76, students apply the procedure of circling the part that names and underlining the part that tells more to sentences in a passage. All the sentences begin with the part that names.

Beginning in lesson 82, students analyze passages to identify the sentences. The sentences have no capitals or periods. Students identify the part that names and the part that tells more to figure out where each sentence starts and ends. They then capitalize the first word and put a period at the end of each sentence. Here's the exercise from lesson 82.

EXERCISE 3   Paragraph Editing

Capitals and Periods

1. Everybody, find part B. ✔
   Somebody forgot to put capitals and periods in the sentences.

2. Look at the first words in the paragraph and figure out what the first sentence names.
- Everybody, what does it name? (Signal.) *A red kite.*
  Circle **a red kite.** ✔
- The first sentence tells more about a red kite. (Call on a student:) Say the rest of the sentence that starts with **a red kite.** *Floated into the sky.*
- Everybody, put a period after the word **sky.** Start the next sentence with a capital **T.** ✔

3. Look at the first words in the second sentence and figure out what that sentence names.

- Everybody, what does it name? (Signal.) *The wind.*
  Circle the wind. ✔
- Everybody, say the words that tell more about the wind. (Signal.) *Blew the kite.*
- Put a period after the word **kite.** Start the next sentence with a capital **T.** ✔
4. Fix up the rest of this paragraph. Make sure each sentence begins with a capital and ends with a period. Circle the part of each sentence that names. Raise your hand when you're finished.
   (Observe students and give feedback.)
- Everybody, what does it name? (Signal.) *The wind.*
  Circle the wind. ✔
- Everybody, say the words that tell more about the wind. (Signal.) *Blew the kite.*
- Put a period after the word **kite.** Start the next sentence with a capital **T.** ✔
4. Fix up the rest of this paragraph. Make sure each sentence begins with a capital and ends with a period. Circle the part of each sentence that names. Raise your hand when you're finished.
   (Observe students and give feedback.)
5. Let's check your work. Make an **X** over anything you missed.
- First sentence: You should have circled **a red kite.** A red kite floated into the sky, period.
- Next sentence: You should have circled **the wind.** Capital **T,** The wind blew the kite, period.
- Next sentence: You should have circled **three brown ducks.** Capital **T,** Three brown ducks flew near the kite, period.
- Next sentence: You should have circled **the kite.** Capital **T,** The kite went behind some clouds, period.
- Next sentence: You should have circled **it.** Capital **I,** It went so high that nobody could see it, period.
6. Raise your hand if you made no mistakes. Great job.
- Everybody else, fix up any mistakes you made in part B.
  (Observe students and give feedback.)

Teaching Notes

This type of exercise is very difficult for students who have not learned to analyze sentences with respect to subject and predicate. Students who understand subject-predicate may still have some problems, but you can correct mistakes by referring to what they know. They learn that placement of capitals and periods is not a random activity.

In later lessons, students fix up passages in which **some** of the sentences do not have capitals or periods. This editing context is similar to the situation in which students write and edit their own work.

In lesson 87, students are taught that the part of the sentence that names is the **subject.** Here's the first part of that exercise.

EXERCISE 3   Subject
1. Pencils down. You're going to learn about the **subject** of a sentence. Listen: The **subject** of a sentence is the part of the sentence that names.
   Everybody, what do we call the part of the sentence that names? (Signal.) *The subject.*
2. Listen: Six little dogs barked loudly. Everybody, what's the part that names? (Signal.) *Six little dogs.*
- So what's the subject of that sentence? (Signal.) *Six little dogs.*
- Listen: A boy and a girl walked in the park. What's the subject of that sentence? (Signal.) *A boy and a girl.*
- Listen: They went home. What's the subject of that sentence? (Signal.) *They.*
- (Repeat step 2 until firm.)
3. Listen: That shirt is beautiful. What's the subject of that sentence? (Signal.) *That shirt.*
- Listen: My mother and her friend talked on the phone. What's the subject of that sentence? (Signal.) *My mother and her friend.*

- Listen: Her face and her hands got dirty. What's the subject of that sentence? (Signal.) *Her face and her hands.*
- (Repeat step 3 until firm.)

Teaching Notes

Sentences are grouped so that you can firm responses (steps 2 and 3). Within each group are greatly different sentences. One has a subject containing more than one word (six little dogs); one has a subject that names more than one entity (a boy and a girl); one has a pronoun for a subject (they). This variation assures that students do not learn serious misrules about the nature of the subject and assume that a subject must have a certain arrangement or number of words. Learning the new word **subject** for the part that names is not difficult for students. They already know the concept (the part that names).

Learning the new label involves no new understanding. It is simply identifying something that is familiar with a new word. Make sure that you firm students in step 2 and step 3 before presenting the written work that follows the oral activity.

In lesson 89, students learn to identify the part that tells more as the **predicate.** In later lessons, students continue to use the subject-predicate skills. Some exercises present sentence parts, and students identify the parts as either subject or predicate. For some exercises, students are presented with subjects in one column and predicates in the second column. They combine the parts to create unique sentences.

Parts of Speech

The parts of speech that are introduced in Grade 2 are verbs and pronouns. The work on both verbs and pronouns begins early in the program (lesson 69); however, students are not taught the labels until much later in the program (lesson 106).

Verb Usage

The analysis of verbs moves in two directions. The first direction involves what the students write. Typically, students overuse sentences with progressive verbs.

They were going to the store.

Often, students have tense shifts.

The man came into the room.
He sits down.

The initial verb activities focus on these tendencies. The pictures that students refer to when writing show what **happened.** To tell about these pictures, students are to indicate what the characters **did,** not what they are doing or were doing.

This work begins in lesson 69. Students are presented with regular present-tense verbs. (The verbs are regular because they can be converted to past-tense verbs by adding **ed.**) Students write the past-tense verbs. Here's the exercise from lesson 69.

WORKBOOK

EXERCISE 2   Suffixes –ed

1. Everybody, pencils down. Open your workbook to lesson 69 and find part A. ✔
2. The words in part A tell what people do. You can make the words tell what people **did** by adding the letters **e-d** to the end of each word. What letters do you add to make the words tell what people did? (Signal.) *E-d.*
3. Touch word 1. ✔
   What word? (Signal.) *Burn.*
   If you add the letters **e-d** to **burn,** the word says **burned.**
4. Touch word 2.
   What word? (Signal.) *Fill.*
- What letters do you add to make the word tell what people did? (Signal.) *E-d.*
- When you add **e-d,** you get a word that tells what people did. That word is **filled.** Spell **filled.** (Signal.) *F-i-l-l-e-d.*

5. Touch word 3.
   What word? (Signal.) *Push.*
   • **Push** tells what people **do.** Say the word that tells what they **did.** (Signal.) *Pushed.*
   • Spell **pushed.** (Signal.) *P-u-s-h-e-d.*

6. Go back to word 1.
   The word that tells what people do is **burn.** What's the word that tells what they did? (Signal.) *Burned.*
   • Write the word **burned** in the blank after **burn.** (Observe students and give feedback.)

7. Touch word 2.
   The word that tells what people do is **fill.** What's the word that tells what they did? (Signal.) *Filled.*
   • Write the word **filled** in the blank after **fill.** (Observe students and give feedback.)

8. Write the rest of the words that tell what people did. Raise your hand when you're finished.
   (Observe students and give feedback.)

9. Let's check your work. Make an **X** next to any item you missed.
   • Everybody, touch item 1.
   Say the word that tells what people did. (Signal.) *Burned.*
   Spell **burned.** (Signal.) *B-u-r-n-e-d.*
   • Touch item 2.
   Say the word that tells what people did. (Signal.) *Filled.*
   Spell **filled.** (Signal.) *F-i-l-l-e-d.*
   • Touch item 3.
   Say the word that tells what people did. (Signal.) *Pushed.*
   Spell **pushed.** (Signal.) *P-u-s-h-e-d.*
   • Touch item 4.
   Say the word that tells what people did. (Signal.) *Licked.*
   Spell **licked.** (Signal.) *L-i-c-k-e-d.*
   • Touch item 5.
   Say the word that tells what people did. (Signal.) *Started.*
   Spell **started.** (Signal.) *S-t-a-r-t-e-d.*
   • Touch item 6.
   Say the word that tells what people did. (Signal.) *Scratched.*
   Spell **scratched.** (Signal.) *S-c-r-a-t-c-h-e-d.*

10. Raise your hand if you got no items wrong. Great job.
    • Raise your hand if you got 1 item wrong. Good work.
    • Fix up any mistakes you made in part A. (Observe students and give feedback.)

Teaching Notes

Students may be weak at spelling the words in step 9. If the responses are weak to the first two items, model the response you expect. Spell the words at a relatively slow rate (about 1/2 second per letter.) If you spell the words very fast, students will not be able to learn from your model.
Go back to item 1. My turn: Spell burned. B-U-R-N-E-D. Your turn: Spell burned. Touch item 2. My turn to spell filled: F-I-L-L-E-D. Your turn: Spell filled.

In lesson 70, students review regular verbs and are introduced to a set of five irregular verbs. Students work with these five irregulars for four lessons. Then another set of irregulars is introduced. The procedure is repeated for three more sets of verbs. The verbs introduced include more common irregulars that students use when they write. Note, however, that the set of verbs is not exhaustive. Here's the student material from lesson 70.

Part B	In each blank, write the word that tells what people did.		
1. find _found_	6. buy _____	11. dig _____
2. give _gave_	7. find _____	12. buy _____
3. buy _bought_	8. dig _____	13. have _____
4. dig _dug_	9. have _____	14. give _____
5. have _had_	10. give _____	15. find _____

In lesson 71, students are presented with sentences that have progressive verbs (*was talking* or *is eating*). Students cross out both words of the verb and write the simple past-tense verb above the crossed-out words. Here's the first part of the exercise from lesson 71.

Part B   Fix up the sentences so they tell what people did.

1. Alice <u>was fixing</u> her bike.

2. The girl <u>was talking</u> loudly.

3. Miss Cook <u>is finding</u> her keys.

4. Her grandmother <u>is smiling</u> at the baby.

5. Mr. Howard <u>was buying</u> a picture.

For things you'll write in this program, you'll tell what people **did,** not what they **were doing** or **are doing.** The words that are underlined in each sentence tell what people were doing or are doing. You're going to fix up those parts to tell what people did.

2. Sentence 1: Alicia was fixing her bike. What words are underlined? (Signal.) *Was fixing.*

• That tells what she was doing. Here's the word that tells what she did: **fixed.** What word tells what she **did?** (Signal.) *Fixed.*

• Sentence 2: The girl was talking loudly. What words are underlined? (Signal.) *Was talking.*

• That tells what she was doing. Everybody, what word tells what she **did?** (Signal.) *Talked.*

• Sentence 3: Miss Cook is finding her keys. What words are underlined? (Signal.) *Is finding.*

• That tells what she is doing. What word tells what she **did?** (Signal.) *Found.*

• Sentence 4: Her grandmother is smiling at the baby. What words are underlined? (Signal.) *Is smiling.*

• That tells what she is doing. What word tells what she **did?** (Signal.) *Smiled.*

• Sentence 5: Mr. Howard was buying a picture. What words are underlined? (Signal.) *Was buying.*

• That tells what he was doing. What word tells what he **did?** (Signal.) *Bought.*

• (Repeat step 2 until firm.)

3. Your turn: Cross out the underlined words in each sentence. Above those words, write the word that tells what people did. Raise your hand when you're finished. (Observe students and give feedback.)

Teaching Notes

Make sure the students are firm on step 2 before they cross out the underlined words and write the simple past-tense verb. If students make mistakes in step 2, immediately tell them the correct answer. Repeat the task that they missed. If they make more than two mistakes in the series, repeat step 2 from the beginning.

Students apply the rule about past-tense verbs to their writing, starting in lesson 9. All sentences they write tell what illustrated characters **did.**

Starting in lesson 80, students discriminate between sentences that tell what people did and sentences that don't tell what they did. Some sentences tell what people were doing; some tell what people did. Students cross out the verbs that don't tell what people did and write the correct verb above it.

ran

He was running.

In lesson 83, students edit a passage for inappropriate verbs. Here's the passage and part of the exercise from lesson 83.

EXERCISE 3   Paragraph Editing

Past Time

1. Everybody, find part B. ✔
I'll read the instructions: Make each sentence tell what a person or thing did.

2. Touch the first sentence.
Mark looked for a hidden treasure. That sentence tells what Mark did.

• I'll read the next sentence: He is going into his backyard with a shovel.
Everybody, does that sentence tell what he did? (Signal.) *No.*

• Say the sentence so it tells what he did. (Signal.) *He went into his backyard with a shovel.*

• Cross out **is going** and write **went** above the crossed-out words. ✔

3. Everybody, touch the check box below the paragraph.

- I'll read the check: Does each sentence tell what a person or thing did?
  The **X**s in the box show how many mistakes there are in the paragraph. Count the **X**s and you'll know how many mistakes you should find. (Pause.)
- Everybody, how many mistakes? (Signal.) *Four.*
- Read the rest of the paragraph. Fix up any sentence that does not tell what Mark or his shovel did. Raise your hand when you're finished.
  (Observe students and give feedback.)

Teaching Notes

The student material has a check followed by four Xs. **Does each sentence tell what a person or thing did? (X X X X.)** The Xs provide you with a method for directing students to read the paragraph carefully. If a student missed one of the sentences, you might say something like, "You found three of the sentences that don't tell what a person or thing did, but there are four Xs. Look for the fourth sentence that is wrong and fix it up."

In the lessons following lesson 83, students work on variations of the editing exercise above. In lesson 85, the Xs are dropped, and students may tend to make the mistake of not finding all the sentences that have the wrong verb. If students get stuck, you may want to tell them how many sentences they overlooked. (Do not point out the improper sentences. You want to make students facile at rereading and correcting what is written.)

In lesson 96, students correct sentences that have verbs such as **bringed, gots, thinked.** The correct verbs for these items are words that students have studied as irregular verbs.

Verbs as Parts of Speech

Starting with lesson 106, students are introduced to the label **verb** and analyze sentences to identify the verbs. Verbs are the first part of speech that students identify. The reason verbs are introduced first is that they are relatively easy for students to identify if they understand subject

and predicate. In all the sentences they will work with, the verb is the first part of the predicate. Note that by using the subject-predicate analysis, students have less difficulty identifying verbs like **had** and **were** even though they don't specify an action.

Here's the introduction from lesson 106. All the sentences have one-word verbs.

EXERCISE 3   Parts Of Speech

Verbs

1. Everybody, pencils down. Remember, every sentence has a verb. The verb is usually in the first part of the predicate.
   - I'm going to say some sentences.
2. Listen: A dog ate lots of food. Say it. (Signal.) *A dog ate lots of food.*
   - What's the subject? (Signal.) *A dog.*
     What's the predicate? (Signal.) *Ate lots of food.*
     What's the first word in the predicate? (Signal.) *Ate.*
   - That's the verb.
   - Listen: The girl threw a ball. Say it. (Signal.) *The girl threw a ball.*
   - What's the subject? (Signal.) *The girl.*
     What's the predicate? (Signal.) *Threw a ball.*
     What's the first word in the predicate? (Signal.) *Threw.*
   - That's the verb.
   - (Repeat step 2 until firm.)
3. Listen: Boys and girls were in school. Say it. (Signal.) *Boys and girls were in school.*
   - What's the subject? (Signal.) *Boys and girls.*
     What's the predicate? (Signal.) *Were in school.*
     What's the verb? (Signal.) *Were.*
   - Listen: A bird flew. Say it. (Signal.) *A bird flew.*
   - What's the subject? (Signal.) *A bird.*
     What's the predicate? (Signal.) *Flew.*
     What's the verb? (Signal.) *Flew.*
   - Yes, **flew.** There's only one word in the predicate, so that word has to be the verb.
   - (Repeat step 3 until firm.)

Part C

1. Six bottles were on the table.
2. An old lion chased the rabbit.
3. Jane and Sue sat under a tree.
4. His brother had a candy bar.

EXERCISE 4   Verbs

1. Everybody, find part C. ✔
2. I'll read sentence 1: Six bottles were on the table. What's the subject? (Signal.) *Six bottles.*
   - What's the predicate? (Signal.) *Were on the table.*
   - What's the verb? (Signal.) *Were.*
   - Sentence 2: An old lion chased the rabbit. What's the subject? (Signal.) *An old lion.*
   - What's the predicate? (Signal.) *Chased the rabbit.*
   - What's the verb? (Signal.) *Chased.*
3. Here are the instructions for part C: Circle the subject of each sentence. Underline the predicate. Then make a **V** above the verb. Remember, the verb is the first word of the predicate. Do the sentences now. Raise your hand when you're finished. (Observe students and give feedback.)

Teaching Notes

Make sure that students are firm on the verbal items in exercise 3 (steps 2 and 3) before you present the written activity in exercise 4.

Pronoun Usage

Just as the verb activities move in two directions (writing and grammatical analysis) the activities that teach pronouns and their usage also go in two directions (writing usage and grammar). The major problem that students experience when using pronouns is that they create sentences that are not clear. The early pronoun activities address this problem with rules and with practice.

The first pronoun activity is introduced in lesson 72. The introduction demonstrates that specific pronouns can be used to replace names or nouns. Here's the introduction.

EXERCISE 4   Pronouns

He and She

1. Everybody, pencils down. Find part C. ✔
   - The person named in each sentence is underlined. You're going to change the underlined part to **he** or **she.**
2. Touch sentence 1.
   The girl was running. Say the part of the sentence that names. (Signal.) *The girl.*
   - Are you going to change **the girl** to **he** or **she?** (Signal.) *She.*
   - Say the sentence with **she.** (Signal.) *She was running.*
3. Touch sentence 2.
   My grandfather read a book. Say the part of the sentence that names. (Signal.) *My grandfather.*
   - Are you going to change **my grandfather** to **he** or **she?** (Signal.) *He.*
   - Say the sentence with **he.** (Signal.) *He read a book.*
4. Touch sentence 1 again.
   Sentence 1 says: The girl was running. We change **the girl** to **she.** Write **she** in the blank. Start with capital **S.**
   (Observe students and give feedback.)
5. Start the rest of the sentences in part C with **he** or **she.** Remember to start each sentence with a capital. Raise your hand when you're finished.
   (Observe students and give feedback.)

Teaching Notes

The initial exercise introduces the idea that the pronoun replaces the entire subject of a sentence—the noun and any words that precede it. Although students have a functional understanding of this substitution game, the set of examples they work with initially makes the nature of pronouns much more understandable than it is when students are taught a rule such as: Pronouns are used in place of nouns.

In lesson 74, students work on an activity similar to the one above except that some of the sentences have subjects that are replaced with **it: This book** was very funny. **It** was very funny.

Starting in lesson 79, students write the appropriate subject for the second sentence in a pair of related sentences.

WORKBOOK

EXERCISE 2   Pronouns

He, She, It

1. Everybody, open your workbook to lesson 79 and find part A. ✔
- Each item tells what the same person or thing did. We don't want to start all the sentences with the same name. So we start the second sentence in each item with **he, she** or **it**.
2. Everybody, touch number 1.
I'll read the first sentence: Robert spent all morning cleaning his room. Everybody, what part of that sentence names? (Signal.) *Robert.*
- The next sentence also tells about Robert. What other word can we use to refer to **Robert?** (Signal.) *He.*
- So here's the next sentence: He put his dirty clothes in the laundry basket.
3. Touch number 2.
I'll read the first sentence: My sister went to the park. Everybody, what part of that sentence names? (Signal.) *My sister.*
- The next sentence also tells about my sister. What other word can we use to refer to **my sister?** (Signal.) *She.*
- So here's the next sentence: She played basketball with her friends for two hours.
4. Touch number 3.
I'll read the first sentence: The boat held four people. Everybody, what part of that sentence names? (Signal.) *The boat.*
- The next sentence also tells about the boat. What other word can we use to refer to **the boat?** (Signal.) *It.*
- So here's the next sentence: It had three sails.

5. Fill in the blanks. Start the second sentence in each item with **he, she** or **it**. Remember to start each sentence with a capital. Raise your hand when you're finished.
(Observe students and give feedback.)

Teaching Notes

About the only problem that students have with these activities is keying off spurious words in the subject. In lesson 70, for instance, one of the items is: **His mother** liked to fix cars. _____ worked in a car shop.
Sometimes, students will key on the word **his** in the first sentence and write "He" at the beginning of the second sentence. The simplest correction for this kind of mistake is to act shocked. "His mother is a he? He has a man for a mother? Wow!"
If you use this kind of correction one time, you'll probably never have to use it again.

In lesson 80, students are introduced to a rule for using pronouns in a passage. The rule: If two sentences in a row name the same thing, you change the second sentence so that it names **he, she,** or **it**.

EXERCISE 3   Pronouns

He, She, It

1. Everybody, pencils down. Find part B. ✔
You're going to change the part that names in some of the sentences to **he, she** or **it**.
2. I'll read the paragraph. Follow along. Susan loved birds. Susan wanted to build a bird house. Her grandfather gave Susan a book about bird houses. Her grandfather told Susan to read it carefully. The book was interesting. The book showed how to build a bird house.
3. Here's the rule for these sentences: If two sentences in a row name the same thing, we change the second sentence so it names **he, she** or **it**. Once more: If two

sentences in a row name the same thing, we change the second sentence so it names **he, she** or **it.**

4. Sentence A names Susan. Look at sentence B. Everybody, who does sentence B name? (Signal.) *Susan.*

- Two sentences in a row name the same person, so we change the second sentence to **he, she** or **it.** Which of those words refers to Susan? (Signal.) *She.*
- Cross out **Susan** in sentence B. Write **she.** Remember to start with a capital. ✔
- Here are the first and second sentences: Susan loved birds. **She** wanted to build a bird house.

5. Now we look at the next sentence. Everybody, who does sentence C name? (Signal.) *Her grandfather.*

- Does that sentence name the same person sentence B names? (Signal.) *No.*
- So we **don't** change sentence C. We don't have two sentences in a row that name the same person. Sentence B refers to **Susan.** Sentence C refers to **her grandfather.**

6. Look at the next sentence—sentence D. Everybody, who does sentence D name? (Signal.) *Her grandfather.*

- Does that sentence name the same person sentence C names? (Signal.) *Yes.*
- So we have two sentences in a row that name the same person—sentence C and sentence D. Everybody, which sentence do you change? (Signal.) *Sentence D.*
- You change **her grandfather** in sentence D to **he, she** or **it.** Which word refers to **her grandfather?** (Signal.) *He.* Change sentence D to **he.** ✔

7. Look at the next sentence—sentence E. Everybody, what does sentence E name? (Signal.) *The book.*

- Does that sentence name the same thing sentence D names? (Signal.) *No.*
- So we don't have to change sentence E. We don't have two sentences in a row that name the same thing.

8. Look at the last sentence—sentence F. Everybody, what does sentence F name? (Signal.) *The book.*

- Does that sentence name the same thing sentence E names? (Signal.) *Yes.*
- They both name the book. So we have two sentences in a row that name the same thing—sentence E and sentence F. Which sentence do you change? (Signal.) *Sentence F.*
- You change **the book** in sentence F to **he, she** or **it.** Which word refers to **the book?** (Signal.) *It.*
- Change sentence F to **it.** ✔

9. I'll read the fixed-up paragraph. Check your work. Susan loved birds. Capital **S, She** wanted to build a bird house. Her grandfather gave Susan a book about bird houses. Capital **H, He** told Susan to read it carefully. The book was interesting. Capital **I, It** showed how to build a bird house.

10. Fix up any mistakes you made in part B. (Observe students and give feedback.)

Teaching Notes

Most students will not have serious problems with this exercise if you follow the wording of the exercise carefully. Don't add extraneous words, rules, or observations.

Sometimes students don't understand that they are supposed to look at two sentences in a row. You can usually spot problems of not understanding by weak responses to the questions that you present in steps 4 through 8. If you get weak responses, direct students to touch the first part of each sentence you name. In step 4, you would say, "Sentence A names **Susan.** Touch that part of the sentence. With your other hand touch the underlined part of Sentence B." Then present the rest of the step as specified. Repeat the same procedure for the rest of the sentences.

Students work variations of the activity above in the following lessons. In lesson 97, they are introduced to a variation involving the pronoun **they.**

Mechanics

In Grade 2 language arts, students learn basic rules for capitalizing and using ending marks.

Capitals and Ending Marks

One of the more serious problems that students have when they write is writing in sentence units. Part of the problem comes from their lack of knowledge about what sentences are. Because they have trouble identifying the sentences they are trying to compose, they understandably have trouble putting capitals at the beginning of sentences and periods or question marks at the end.

The first work with capitals and periods begins in lesson 66. Students copy sentences or complete isolated sentences. For both activities they capitalize the first word and put a period at the end of each sentence.

Starting in lesson 82 (after students have learned the basic subject-predicate analysis for declarative sentences), the work on capitals and periods focuses more on identifying sentences in a passage. The first activity involves a paragraph that has no capitals and no periods. Students use the subject-predicate analysis to identify the sentences, then capitalize the first word and mark the end with a period.

A variation of this activity is presented in lesson 89. For this variation, some sentences lack capitals, some lack periods, and some are correct. Here's the student activity from lesson 89.

Part A | Put in the missing capitals and periods.

every student in the class read a book Tom and Alice read a book about animals they learned about animals that live in different parts of the world Two students read a book about roses that book told how to take care of roses.

Teaching Notes

Remember, the purpose of this teaching is to help students when they write. If students write in non-sentences, take them through the basic steps for figuring out how to make their sentences mechanically correct. Ask, "What's the subject? . . . What's the predicate? . . . Now that you know the sentence, you can put in the capital at the beginning and the period at the end." (If the sentence the student writes is not a type that had been introduced in Level C, simply show the student where the capital and period go.)

In lesson 94, students are introduced to a rule about persons' names. The rule: Each part of a person's name begins with a capital. This rule helps students with otherwise complicated names such as "Mister Henry Jackson."

Editing

Part of the transition from skill learning to writing is editing. Each skill or convention is first taught as a relatively simple rule or procedure. Next, students **edit** passages for violations of the "rule" that had been taught. The violations that are presented are typically mistakes that naive writers make. Finally, students apply the rule in their own writing.

Editing activities begin in lesson 95 and continue to the end of Grade 2. The activities present many of the mistakes that students make when they write. Editing the mistakes written by somebody else is far easier for students than dealing with mistakes in their own writing. The repeated practice in editing mistakes of others makes it easier for students to read and edit their own work.

Here's an early editing activity (lesson 37) in which students edit for sentences that begin with **And** or **And then.**

Part B Fix up the mistakes in each item.

1. Tom and I was both born on the first wednesday in december. (3)

2. Janes hand got dirty, when she planted trees (3)

3. Ann visited her grandmother every monday night in april and may. (3)

4. Cats and dogs was running in Toms yard. (2)

5. Alex and i were talking to cora. (2)

6. Kay asked her dad can i stay up late? (5)

7. When mr. adams got home on Thursday. He read the newspaper. (4)

Writing
Reporting

Nearly all writing assignments in Grade 2 language arts are referenced to pictures. Students **report** on what a picture shows. The sentences they write have a past-tense verb. Accompanying the later writing exercises are checks. The checks indicate the major criteria the writing should achieve. The checks vary from assignment to assignment. Also, they become more "inclusive" as students progress through the program. Earlier checks are specific, such as, "Does each sentence begin with a capital and end with a period?" A check later in the program would be, "Are all your sentences written correctly?" This check implies checking the sentence for various mechanical criteria and logical details.

Reporting exercises that teach the discrimination between **reporting** and **inferring** are reviewed at the beginning of Part II.

Main Idea

Beginning in lesson 71, students select sentences that tell the main thing illustrated characters did. This exercise is important because, when students "report" by naming a character and telling what the character did, they are expected to describe the main thing the character did.

EXERCISE 6 Main Idea

1. Everybody, take out a sheet of lined paper and write your name on the top line. Then number your lined paper 1 and 2. Raise your hand when you're finished. ✔
- Everybody, pencils down. Open your textbook to lesson 71 and find part E. ✔
2. Touch picture 1.
   One of the sentences next to the picture tells the main thing the person did. The other sentences tell about a detail.
- First sentence: Mary held a glass. Say that sentence. (Signal.) *Mary held a glass.*
- My turn: That's not the **main thing** Mary did. That's a **detail.**
- Next sentence: Mary drank a glass of water. Say that sentence. (Signal.) *Mary drank a glass of water.*
- That's the **main thing** Mary did.
- Next sentence: Mary wore a belt. Say that sentence. (Signal.) *Mary wore a belt.*
- Everybody, is that the **main thing** Mary did or **a detail?** (Signal.) *A detail.*
3. Touch picture 2.
   One of these sentences tells the **main thing** the person did. The other sentences tell about **a detail.**
4. First sentence: Jill bent her leg. Say that sentence. (Signal.) *Jill bent her leg.*
- Everybody, is that the **main thing** Jill did or **a detail?** (Signal.) *A detail.*
- Next sentence: Jill held the board with one hand. Say that sentence. (Signal.) *Jill held the board with one hand.*
- Everybody, is that the main thing Jill did or a detail? (Signal.) *A detail.*
- Next sentence: Jill sawed a board. Say that sentence. (Signal.) *Jill sawed a board.*
- Everybody, is that the main thing Jill did or a detail? (Signal.) *The main thing.*
- (Repeat step 4 until firm.)

5. I'll read the instructions for part E: For each picture, copy the sentence that tells the main thing the person did. Don't copy any of the other sentences. You have two minutes. Raise your hand when you're finished.
   (Observe students and give feedback.)

Starting in lesson 74, students compose sentences that tell the main thing characters did. This exercise is the first in which students check their work for various criteria.

EXERCISE 5 Main Idea

1. Everybody, take out a sheet of lined paper. Write your name on the top line. Number the paper 1 through 2. Raise your hand when you're finished.
   • Everybody, pencils down. Open your textbook to lesson 74 and find part D. ✔
2. The rule in the box for part D tells about sentences that report on the main thing a person did. Touch that rule. ✔
   • I'll read: Sentences that report on the main thing a person did have two parts. The first part of the sentence **names the person.** The second part **tells the main thing the person did.** Remember, the first part names; the second part tells more.
3. You're going to say sentences that report on the main thing each person did. Remember, when you report, you can only tell what the picture shows.
   • Everybody, touch picture 1. Name the person in that picture. (Signal.) *Beth.*
   • Get ready to say a sentence that reports on the main thing Beth **did.** Don't say what Beth **is doing** or **was doing.** Start by naming Beth. Then tell the main thing Beth **did.** (Call on a student. Praise sentences

such as: *Beth painted the ceiling.* For each good sentence: Everybody, say that sentence.)
4. Everybody, touch picture 2. Name that person. (Signal.) *Rosa.*
   • Get ready to say a sentence that reports on the main thing Rosa did. Don't say what Rosa **is doing** or **was doing.** Make up a sentence that tells the main thing Rosa **did.** (Call on a student. Praise sentences such as: *Rosa read a book.* For each good sentence: Everybody, say that sentence.)
5. Touch the words in the vocabulary box as I read them: **painted, book, ceiling, read.** Be sure to spell those words correctly if you use them.
6. I'll read the instructions for part D. Write a sentence that reports on the main thing each person did.
   • Next to number 1 on your paper, write a sentence that reports on what the person in picture 1 did. Do the same thing for picture 2. Be sure each sentence starts with a capital and ends with a period. You have 3 minutes. Raise your hand when you're finished.
   (Observe students and give feedback.)
7. (After 3 minutes, say:) Stop writing. If you didn't finish, you can write the rest of the sentences at the end of the lesson.
8. I'll call on students to read their sentences. Listen to each sentence and see if it **names** the right person and tells **the main thing** that person **did.** (Call on individual students to read the sentences they wrote for pictures 1 and 2. After each good sentence, tell the group:) Everybody, say that sentence.
9. (Write on the board:)

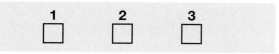

   • Let's check your work. These are check boxes. Make boxes like these below your last sentence.
   (Observe students and give feedback.)
10. Everybody, touch the box for check 1.
    • Here's check 1: Does each sentence begin with a capital and end with a period?

- Read your sentences. If they begin with a capital and end with a period, put a check mark like this in box 1 on your paper. (Make a check mark in box 1.)
- If you forgot any capitals or periods, fix up your sentences now and then make the check mark. Don't make a check mark until you've checked your sentences and fixed up any mistakes. Raise your hand when you're finished.
  (Observe students and give feedback.)

11. Now touch the box for check 2 on your paper.
- Here's check 2: Does each sentence tell the main thing the person did?
- Read over your sentences carefully. Each sentence should start out by naming the person. Then it should tell the main thing the person did. When all your sentences name and tell the main thing the person did, put a check mark in box 2. Raise your hand when you're finished.
  (Observe students and give feedback.)

12. Now touch the box for check 3.
- Here's that check: Did you spell words from the vocabulary box correctly?
- Look at each sentence. Make sure vocabulary words are spelled correctly. Fix up any mistakes and make a check mark in box 3. Raise your hand when you're finished.
  (Observe students and give feedback.)

13. Raise your hand if you think you'll get a **super** paper.
- I'll read your sentences later and hand them back at the beginning of the next lesson. I'll mark any mistakes I find.
- Also on the next lesson, you'll have a test. Here's the rule about the test: If you don't make any more than 2 mistakes on the test, you'll get a **super** on your test.

Teaching Notes

Steps 6 through 12 are particularly important. In step 6, make sure that you circulate among the students. Praise the students who are working quickly and accurately. Make sure

that others can hear your comments. If students are working slowly, warn them that they don't have unlimited time. "In about one more minute, you'll have to stop writing, so try to finish up."

When you tell students to stop writing (step 7), make sure they stop writing.

The general rules for conducting the checks and making them important to the students and effective for instruction are detailed on page 25 of the guide. Follow these procedures (or a variation of them) starting with lesson 74.

After directing each check, circulate among the students and see if they are following the check procedure. Do not "mother hen" them if you observe a mistake. If a student has a check mark in box one but has a mistake, tell the student, "You didn't fix up all your sentences so that they begin with a capital and end with a period. Read your sentences over very carefully. Find the sentence that's wrong and fix it up."

Remember, the more you show the students the mistakes they made and show them how to fix them up, the less some of them will listen to you when you're trying to instruct them.

Also, keep the checks moving fast. When the students have had a reasonable amount of time for check one (half a minute), present check two, or present the "random test" procedure described on page 90 for determining the points the group receives. Remember, the checks teach the students a great deal about writing. If the checks are done effectively, students will actually do them. If not, some will fake it.

Paragraph Writing

Starting in lesson 84, students work on a paragraph. The first sentence is written. That sentence tells the main thing a group of people did. Students then write a sentence for each illustrated character. These sentences tell the main thing each character did.

EXERCISE 6 Paragraph Writing

Groups

1. Everybody, take out a sheet of lined paper and write your name on the top line. Raise your hand when you're finished.

• Open your textbook to lesson 84 and find part E. ✔

2. Everybody, touch the words in the vocabulary box as I read them: **hammer, side, board, nail, saw, paint.** Be sure to spell those words correctly if you use them.

3. I'll read the instructions: Write a paragraph. Copy the sentence that tells the main thing the group did. Then write three more sentences. Write one sentence about each person. Tell the main thing each person did.

4. Everybody, touch Kay.

• Raise your hand when you can say a sentence that reports on the main thing Kay did. (Call on several students. Praise sentences such as: *Kay hammered a nail into a board on the side of the house.* For each good sentence: Everybody, say that sentence.)

5. Everybody, touch Milly.

• Raise your hand when you can say a sentence that reports on the main thing Milly did. (Call on several students. Praise sentences such as: *Milly sawed a board.* For each good sentence: Everybody, say that sentence.)

6. Everybody, touch Jean.

• Raise your hand when you can say a sentence that reports on the main thing Jean did. (Call on several students. Praise sentences such as: *Jean painted the side of the house with a paintbrush.* For each good sentence: Everybody, say that sentence.)

7. The sentence that tells the main thing the group did is written under the picture. Everybody, read that sentence. (Signal.) *The women worked on the house.*

• Everybody, copy that sentence. Remember to indent. Raise your hand when you're finished. (Observe students and give feedback.)

8. Now you're going to write a sentence about each of the women. Touch Kay.

• Listen: Write a sentence that names Kay and tells the main thing she did. Start that sentence right after the period of the first sentence. Raise your hand when you're finished. (Observe students and give feedback.)

9. Touch Milly in the picture.

• Write a sentence that names Milly and tells the main thing she did. Remember to start that sentence right after the period of the last sentence. Raise your hand when you're finished. (Observe students and give feedback.)

10. Now write a sentence that names Jean and tells the main thing she did. Remember to start that sentence right after the period. Raise your hand when you're finished. (Observe students and give feedback.)

11. I'm going to call on several students to read their paragraph. Let's see who the good listeners are. Each paragraph starts with the sentence about the group. Then it should have a sentence about Kay, a sentence about Milly, and a sentence about Jean. Each of these sentences should tell the main thing that person did.

• If you hear a mistake, raise your hand. If a sentence is missing, raise your hand. If a sentence doesn't tell the main thing one of the women did, raise your hand. Listen carefully.

12. (Call on a student:) Read your paragraph. When you read it, stop at the end of each sentence so everybody can think about whether that sentence is right. (Praise the paragraph if it has no mistakes.)

13. (Call on several other students to read their paragraph. Praise good paragraphs.)

14. You're going to fix up your paragraph before you hand it in. Make 2 check boxes under your paragraph.

15. Here's check 1: Does each sentence begin with a capital and end with a period? Read each sentence you wrote and fix up any mistakes. Then make a check in box 1. Raise your hand when you're finished with check 1.
(Observe students and give feedback.)

16. Here's check 2: Does each sentence tell the main thing the person did? Make sure you have a sentence for each person and it tells the main thing the person did. Then make a check in box 2. Raise your hand when you're finished with check 2.
(Observe students and give feedback.)

17. Raise your hand if you think you'll get a **super** paper. We'll see next time.

Teaching Notes

Follow the procedures in step 9 very closely. Enforce the idea that the reader is to stop at the end of each sentence. Don't accept poorly worded sentences. If a student reads, "Milly held a saw," prompt the group to identify the problem. (The sentence doesn't tell the main thing Milly did.)
Following each error, use the correction procedure in the shaded box. Praise students that have acceptable sentences.

Beginning in lesson 83, students write a paragraph about a group. They first write a sentence that tells the main thing the **group** did. Then they write two sentences about each member of the group. The first sentence tells the main thing the **character** did. The second sentence tells something else about that character. Here's the first part of the activity.

Sentences that report on the main thing a person did have two parts. The first part of the sentence names the person. The second part tells the main thing the person did.

Write a sentence that reports on the main thing each person did.

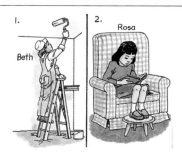

| painted | book | ceiling | read |

Check 1
Does each sentence begin with a capital and end with a period?

Check 2
Does each sentence tell the main thing the person did?

Check 3
Did you spell words from the vocabulary box correctly?

- I'll read the instructions: Write a paragraph that reports on the picture. Begin with a good sentence that tells what the painters did. Then write two sentences about each person. The first sentence should tell the main thing the person did. The second sentence should tell something else about the person.

2. Touch the words in the vocabulary box as I read them: room, ceiling, painted, bottom, roller, kneeled, knees, brushed, ladder, used. Be sure to spell those words correctly if you use them.

3. Write a good sentence that tells the main thing the painters did. Raise your hand when you're finished.
(Observe students and give feedback.)

- (Call on several students to read their sentence. Praise sentences such as: *The painters painted the room.*)

4. Now write two sentences about Jim. Remember, the first sentence names Jim. The second sentence starts with **he.** Raise your hand when you're finished.
(Observe students and give feedback.)

- (Call on several students to read their sentences about Jim. Praise sentences that are consistent with the picture.)

5. Everybody, now you're going to write two sentences about Susan. What word will the second sentence about Susan start with? (Signal.) *She.*

- Write your sentences about Susan. Raise your hand when you're finished. (Observe students and give feedback.)

Teaching Notes

Some of the second sentences may be a little stilted but acceptable. Others are not acceptable. These second sentences for Jim would be acceptable:

> He used a paint brush.
> He kneeled on newspapers.

Here are second sentences that are unacceptable because they refer to details that are irrelevant or redundant:

> He wore shoes.
> He looked at the wall.
> He used paint.

In lesson 101, students write a paragraph about a series of pictures.

LINED PAPER

EXERCISE 5 Paragraph Writing

1. Everybody, take out a sheet of lined paper. Write your name on the top line. ✔

- Everybody, pencils down. Find part D in your textbook. ✔
  I'll read the instructions: Write a paragraph that reports on what happened. Write a sentence for each name shown in the pictures.

2. Everybody, touch number 1. ✔
   Name that animal. (Signal.) *A bluebird.*

- Raise your hand when you can say a sentence that reports on the main thing a bluebird did in that picture. (Call on several students. Praise sentences such as: *A bluebird sat on a branch of a tree.* For each good sentence:) Everybody, say that sentence.

3. Everybody, touch number 2. ✔
   Name that animal. (Signal.) *A striped cat.*

- Raise your hand when you can say a sentence that reports on the main thing a striped cat did in that picture. (Call on several students. Praise sentences such as: *A striped cat ran up the trunk of the tree.* For each good sentence:) Everybody, say that sentence.

4. Everybody, touch number 3. ✔
   Name that animal. (Signal.) *The cat.*

- Raise your hand when you can say a sentence that reports on the main thing the cat did in that picture. (Call on several students. Praise sentences such as: *The cat walked out on the branch toward the bird.* For each good sentence:) Everybody, say that sentence.

5. Everybody, touch number 4. ✔
   Name that animal. (Signal.) *The bird.*

- Raise your hand when you can say a sentence that reports on the main thing the bird did in that picture. (Call on several students. Praise sentences such as: *The bird flew into the air.* For each good sentence:) Everybody, say that sentence.

6. Everybody, touch number 5. ✔
   Name that object. (Signal.) *The branch.*

- Raise your hand when you can say a sentence that reports on the main thing the branch did in that picture. (Call on several students. Praise sentences such as: *The branch broke.* For each good sentence:) Everybody, say that sentence.

7. Everybody, touch number 6. ✔
   Name that animal. (Signal.) *The cat.*
   • Raise your hand when you can say a sentence that reports on the main thing the cat did in that picture. (Call on several students. Praise sentences such as: *The cat fell toward the ground.* For each good sentence:) Everybody, say that sentence.

8. I'll read a passage that reports on what happened: A bluebird sat on a branch of a tree. A striped cat ran up the trunk of the tree. The cat walked out on the branch toward the bird. The bird flew into the air. The branch broke. The cat fell toward the ground.

9. I'll say those sentences again.
   • A bluebird sat on the branch of a tree. Say that sentence. (Signal.) *A bluebird sat on the branch of a tree.*
   • A striped cat ran up the trunk of the tree. Say that sentence. (Signal.) *A striped cat ran up the trunk of the tree.*
   • The cat walked out on the branch toward the bird. Say that sentence. (Signal.) *The cat walked out on the branch toward the bird.*
   • The bird flew into the air. Say that sentence. (Signal.) *The bird flew into the air.*
   • The branch broke. Say that sentence. (Signal.) *The branch broke.*
   • The cat fell toward the ground. Say that sentence. (Signal.) *The cat fell toward the ground.*

10. Touch the words in the vocabulary box as I read them: ground, climbed, flew, jumped, landed, broke, trunk, branch.

11. Touch number 1 in the first picture. Name that animal. (Signal.) *A bluebird.*
    • Write a sentence that tells the main thing a bluebird did in the picture. This sentence is the first one in your paragraph, so be sure to indent. Raise your hand when you're finished.
    (Observe students and give feedback.)

12. Touch number 2.
    Name that animal. (Signal.) *A striped cat.*
    • Write a sentence that tells the main thing a striped cat did in the picture. Don't write any numbers. Start writing the sentence

about the striped cat just after the period. Raise your hand when you're finished. (Observe students and give feedback.)

13. Touch number 3.
    Name that animal. (Signal.) *The cat.*
    • Write a sentence that tells the main thing the cat did in that picture. Raise your hand when you're finished.
    (Observe students and give feedback.)

14. Touch number 4.
    Name that animal. (Signal.) *The bird.*
    • Finish your paragraph. Write a clear sentence for each of the names in the pictures. You'll write sentences for names 4, 5 and 6. Raise your hand when you're finished.
    (Observe students and give feedback.)

15. I'm going to call on several students to read their paragraphs. Listen carefully. Make sure each sentence tells the main thing. Make sure no sentences are missing. And make sure each sentence tells what somebody or something did. Raise your hand if you hear a mistake.
    • (Call on several students to read their paragraphs. Praise good paragraphs.)

16. Now you're going to check your paragraph. Make 3 check boxes under your paragraph. ✔

17. Check 1: Does each sentence begin with a capital and end with a period? Check your paragraph. Fix up any mistakes. Then make a check in box 1. Raise your hand when you're finished.
    (Observe students and give feedback.)

18. Check 2: Does each sentence tell the main thing? Read your paragraph. Make sure each sentence tells the main thing. Fix up any mistakes. Then make a check in box 2. Raise your hand when you're finished.
    (Observe students and give feedback.)

19. Check 3: Does each sentence tell what somebody or something **did?** Remember, you can't tell what somebody or something was doing. You have to tell what they did. Fix up any mistakes. Then make a check in box 3. Raise your hand when you're finished.
    (Observe students and give feedback.)

20. Next time, I'll read some of the **super** paragraphs to you.

Teaching Notes

Students are not to write numbers when they write the paragraph. The numbers are guides to the order of the sentences.

As students learn new skills, the assignments for story writing become more elaborate. After students have learned to write sentences that contain direct quotes, students write passages that include direct quotes.

Writing with Clarity

The two main skills emphasized in the clarity activities are **describing the details** that distinguish one thing from similar objects and **using more specific words** instead of general words.

The basic rationale for including specific details is to give the reader a clear picture of the intended event or object.

Here's an early exercise (lesson 93) that requires students to describe specified pictures.

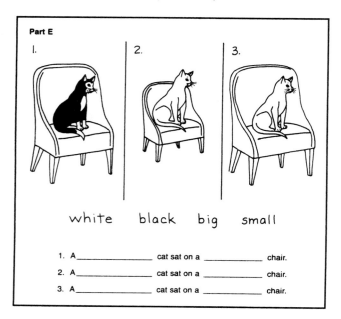

Part E

white   black   big   small

1. A_____ cat sat on a _____ chair.
2. A_____ cat sat on a _____ chair.
3. A_____ cat sat on a _____ chair.

In this exercise, students use adjectives to create sentences that are clear. In similar exercises,

students use phrases that tell where someone or something was. (The house had a window on either side of the door.)

Starting in lesson 97, students are introduced to the need for specific, rather than general, words. The clarity exercise presents a paragraph that could generate many possible "pictures" because the words are general. The general words are underlined. Students indicate why each word is too general and then rewrite the paragraph with specific words. Here's the first part of the exercise from lesson 97.

EXERCISE 5   Paragraph Clarity

1. Everybody, pencils down. Find part D. ✔ Here's a rule about good writing: Good writing tells about things so that you can get a clear picture of what happened. The paragraph in part D has words that are unclear because they don't give us a good picture. The unclear words are underlined.

2. I'll read the first sentence: An animal fell out of a large old tree. The unclear words are **an animal.** We don't know what kind of animal to get a picture of. So we could all get different pictures.

   • What kind of animal do you think fell out of a large old tree? (Call on several students. After each suggested animal, say:) Yes, that's an animal. So that's one of the pictures you could get from the first sentence.

3. Next sentence: It landed on the soft ground. We can get a picture of the soft ground.

4. Next sentence: A person picked it up. The words **a person** are underlined. (Call on a student:) Why? (Praise a response that expresses the idea: *We don't know what kind of person.*)

   • We can get pictures of different persons. I could get a picture of an old man with a long beard.

   • What other kind of person could you picture? (Call on several students. After each suggested person, say:) Yes, that's a person. So that's one of the pictures you could get from that sentence.

5. Last sentence: The person put it in a container and took it home. You could get pictures of a lot of different persons and a lot of different containers.

- What are some containers the person might have used? (Call on several students. After each suggested container, say:) Yes, that's a container. So that's one of the pictures you could get from that sentence.

LINED PAPER • TEXTBOOK

6. Everybody, take out a sheet of lined paper and write your name on the top line. Raise your hand when you're finished. ✔

- Pencils down. Open your textbook to lesson 97 and find part D. ✔

7. The picture shows what happened. You can see what kind of animal fell out of a tree. You can see the person who picked it up. You can see what kind of container the person put it in.

- You're going to rewrite the paragraph so it lets anybody reading the paragraph get a clear picture of what happened. When you rewrite it, you don't want to call the snake just **a snake.** Call it a **big** snake or **striped** snake.
- You don't want to call the person who picked it up just **a girl.** What could you call that person so somebody could get a clear picture of her? (Call on several students. Ideas: *A young girl; a girl wearing cowgirl clothes.*)
- What are you going to call the container? (Call on several students. Ideas: *A wooden basket.*)

8. I'll read the words in the vocabulary box. Follow along: **snake, striped, large, wooden, cowgirl, wearing, boots, outfit, young, basket.**

9. Who can say the first sentence with the underlined part changed so it gives a clear picture of the animal? (Call on several students. Praise sentences such as: *A huge striped snake fell out of a large old tree.* For each good sentence:) Everybody, say that sentence.

- The next sentence says, "It landed on the soft ground." No part is underlined.
- Next sentence. A person picked it up. Who can say that sentence with the underlined part changed so the sentence gives a clear picture of the person? (Call on several students. Praise sentences such as: *A young girl in a cowgirl suit picked it up.* For each good sentence:) Everybody, say that sentence.
- Next sentence. The person put it in a container and took it home. Who can say that sentence with the underlined parts changed so the sentence gives a clear picture of the person and the container? (Call on several students. Praise sentences such as: *The girl put it in a wooden basket and took it home.* For each good sentence:) Everybody, say that sentence.

10. Your turn: Rewrite the paragraph on your lined paper. Remember, change the underlined parts so they give a clear picture. Copy the rest of each sentence. You have 7 minutes. Raise your hand when you're finished.
    (Observe students and give feedback.)

11. (After 7 minutes, say:) Stop writing. I'm going to call on several students to read their paragraphs. Remember, the only parts of the sentences that should be changed are the underlined parts. The new parts should give a clear picture of what happened. Listen carefully and raise your hand if a sentence is wrong or if it doesn't give a clear picture.

- (Call on several students to read their paragraphs. After each paragraph is read, ask the students:) Does that paragraph give a clear picture? (Praise paragraphs that have clear replacements for the underlined words.)

Following the part of the exercise shown above, students check their work for capitals and periods and judge whether each sentence gives a clear picture of what happened.

In later exercises, students edit paragraphs for unclear parts. They refer to a picture for the specific detail that should be in the paragraph. Here's the student material from lesson 101.

Part C

Part D

1. Write a description about picture 1. Tell where the girls were and what they were doing.

2. Write a description about picture 2. Tell where the girls were and what they were doing.

IN-PROGRAM TESTS

The in-program tests that appear as every tenth lesson of the program in part I and every tenth lesson in part II, beginning on lesson 65 provide a basis for periodically judging the progress of individual students and for awarding grades. During a test, students should be seated so they cannot copy.

Directions for presenting the test appear as part of each test lesson.

When observing students's performance, make sure that they are following directions, but do not tell them answers to any item or give them hints.

Collect student workbooks and mark the tests. If students do poorly on a test, check their work on preceding lessons to determine whether they had problems with the tested concepts when they were presented earlier in the program. Also note discrepancies. If a student does poorly on a test, but did very well on all preceding exercises, the student may have been copying.

Mark each item a student misses on the test. Use the Answer Key as the guide. Any deviations are mistakes.

Count the number of mistakes and enter the number at the top of each student's test. If the student missed three items, the score is -3.

Before returning the test forms, use your copy of the Reproducible Group Summary Sheet that appears on page 96 for part I and page 97 for part II and enter the number of errors each student made.

Test Remedies—Part I

Test remedies are appropriate for students who miss test items. It is possible to use formulas for administering test remedies (if 30% of the students miss an item, present the remedy); however, the goal of the remedies would be to fix up each student's misunderstanding. Students who make more than one mistake on any part of the test should receive a remedy for that part. One procedure for doing this is to:

1. Repeat an exercise in the program (from one of the preceding 9 lessons) that deals with the difficult skill.

2. Then present the test again or the part of the test on which students had trouble.

The following is a list of exercises that should be repeated for the various parts of the tests. Although the workbook is copyrighted and may not normally be reproduced, you may reproduce the parts of the workbook needed for test remedies. After firming students on the remedies, repeat the test or the part of the test the student failed.

Test	Test Part Failed	To Remedy, Present: Lesson	To Remedy, Present: Excercise
1 **Lesson 10**	A: Writing Parallel Sentences	Lesson 9	Exercise 2
	B: Right/Left	Lesson 9	Exercise 4
	C: True/False	Lesson 4	Exercise 2
2 **Lesson 20**	A: Writing Parallel Sentences	Lesson 16	Exercise 1
	B: Directions (N, S, E, W)	Lesson 14	Exercise 3
3 **Lesson 30**	A: Writing Parallel Sentences	Lesson 24	Exercise 1
	B: Directions: (N, S, E, W)	Lesson 27	Exercise 1
	C: Deductions	Lesson 28	Exercise 2
4 **Lesson 40**	A: Writing Parallel Sentences	Lesson 24	Exercise 1
	B: Directions (N, S, E, W)	Lesson 38	Exercise 2
	C: Temporal Sequencing	Lesson 34	Exercise 3
	D: Classification	Lesson 33	Exercise 3
5 **Lesson 50**	A: Sentence Writing	Lesson 48	Exercise 2
	B: Directions (N, S, E, W)	Lesson 47	Exercise 1
6 **Lesson 60**	A: Writing Bleep Talk	Lesson 57	Exercise 4
	B: Reporting	Lesson 57	Exercise 1

Test Remedies—Part II

Test remedies are specified as part of each test lesson (under the heading **Test Remedies)**. The criterion for determining whether or not students need a remedy is the percentage of students that make mistakes on a particular part of the test. The criteria are specified as part of the test lesson. Typically, the criteria are stated like this:

If more than 1/4 of the students make 2 or more errors in part _____, present the following exercises. (A list follows.)

The remedies indicate what you should do if the class has problems; however, the guidelines for providing remedies are quite general. Here are more specific guidelines.

1. If students perform poorly on a test, they will probably have trouble on later exercises in the program and should be given a remedy before the next lesson is presented.

2. In many classrooms, the same students tend to perform poorly on different tests; if those are the only students who perform poorly, do not present the remedy to the entire class. If possible, present the remedy only to the students who need it.

3. If it's not possible to schedule a time for providing the remedy to a small group of students (and not the entire class) give the students who performed well a writing assignment similar to the ones on the lessons preceding the test. As they work on the assignment, present the remedies to the students who need additional help.

4. If more than one-fourth of the students have trouble with a part of the test, present the remedy for that part to all students. Then present the lesson following the test.

5. If more than one-fourth of students repeatedly make an unacceptably high number of errors on the tests, try to analyze what's wrong. Possibly, the students should not be placed in Level C. Possibly, they are not trying very hard.

6. Use effective enforcement practices to prompt harder work and better performance. A good guide is *The Solution Book* by Randall Sprick. This text, published by SRA, contains specific suggestions for increasing student motivation. A test summary sheet appears on page 130 A.

REPRODUCIBLE GROUP SUMMARY SHEET—
SUMMARY OF ERRORS

Names	Test 1				Test 2			Test 3				Test 4					Test 5			Test 6		
	A	B	C	Total	A	B	Total	A	B	C	Total	A	B	C	D	Total	A	B	Total	A	B	Total

Names	Test 7					Test 8					Test 9					Test 10				
	A	B	C	D	Total	A	B	C	D	Total	A	B	C	D	Total	A	B	C	D	Total

Objectives

Part I

The objectives on pages 99 to 104 show the development of skills and applications taught in Grade 2 Language Arts program.

The skills and applications are grouped by tracks. The headings indicate the major tracks and the divisions within each track. Each track shows the development of a major topic, such as Story Grammar or Deductions. Typically, a track will have activities that are presented over many different lessons of the program.

The major tracks in Part 1 are:
            CLASSIFICATION AND CLUES
            SENTENCE CONSTRUCTION
DIRECTIONS (North, South, East, West)
            DIALECT
            DEDUCTIONS
            PERSPECTIVE
            TEMPORAL SEQUENCING
            CLARITY
            REPORTING
            WRITING
            STORY GRAMMAR

There are divisions within some tracks. Each division is marked by a subheading.

The subheadings for Dialect are
            CORRECTING
            CREATING AND DISCRIMINATING

The subheadings for Perspective are
            RELATIVE SIZE
            RELATIVE DIRECTION

The subheadings for Clarity are
            CORRECTING AMBIGUITY
            CREATING AMBIGUITY
            DISCRIMINATING

The subheadings for Writing are
            WRITING PARALLEL SENTENCES
            CONSTRUCTING SENTENCES
            COMPOSING SIMPLE STORIES
            ALPHABETIZING SKILLS
            LETTER WRITING
            REPORTING

The subheadings for Story Grammar are
            MODEL STORIES
            APPLICATION
            EXTRAPOLATION

Although the objectives show the various categories and the lessons in which each specific objective is taught, the objectives do not show the interrelationships among the various skills. Specific skills are involved in more than one track. Discrete activities address the teaching of spatial orientation (directions—north, south, east, west), relative direction, relative size, and clarity. However, many activities in the program are difficult to "categorize" because they involve an integration of various skills that are taught.

The story activities present complex perspectives, some of which are not stated objectives. The Goober stories, for instance, present a counterpoint of opposites. Goober is a sensual paradox. (His farm sends out awful smells but also sounds of beautiful music.) The story presents a counterpoint of relative direction. (If the wind blows from the east, the awful odor drifts to the west of his farm.) The Goober stories also present a counterpoint of intent and dialect. People hold their nose in the presence of Goober's farm. What they say is therefore different from what they intend. "You bake dice busic" is not what the speaker is trying to say.

Other stories develop perspectives of relative size (Owen and the Little People), relative distance and direction (Dooly the Duck), clarity of expression (Zelda the Artist), and conclusions about unobserved events (Sherlock and Bertha). All these stories also present perspectives based on motives of different characters.

In summary, the objectives show the various skills and applications that are taught; however, skills and applications developed in one track invariably spill over into other tracks as students use and apply what they have learned.

Review

	Objectives	Lessons
All, Some, None	Answer questions involving **all, some** and **none.**	1
	Fix up pictures to show a true **some** statement.	1, 5
	Fix up pictures to show a true **all** statement.	2, 3
	Cross out objects to make an **all** statement true.	4
	Cross out picture elements to show a true **none** statement.	6
	Write **some** and **none** to complete sentences.	6
	Fix up pictures to show a true **some** statement.	7
If-Then	Apply an if-then rule.	1, 2
	Construct and apply 2 related if-then rules.	8, 9
Left/Right	Follow directions involving **left** or **right.**	1, 2, 5
	Identify letters or objects that are 1st, 2nd, or 3rd to the **left** or **right.**	3, 9
True/False	Circle the words **true** or **false** for statements.	1, 5, 7
Seasons	Identify seasons from descriptions.	11–13

Classification and Clues

Determine which clue eliminates specific members of a class.	2
Use clues to eliminate specific members of a class.	3, 4
Write appropriate object names under class headings.	5, 7
Develop 2 clues that identify a "mystery" object.	6
Use clues to identify members of a class.	22, 23
Arrange objects in larger and smaller classes.	24, 27
Answer questions about mentally-constructed classes.	32–34
Indicate the number of objects in larger and smaller classes.	35
Write 3 sentences to identify the mystery character.	60–63
Write 4 sentences to identify the mystery character.	64, 65

OBJECTIVES FOR PART I, LESSONS 1–65

Writing

Objectives	Lessons
Write parallel sentences	1–
Construct sentences for different illustrations.	3, 7, 11, 12, 44–47
Construct 3 sentences about story characters.	13, 15, 17
Compose 3 simple stories, each based on the same action topic	21, 26, 31
Write a group of sentences that are thematically related.	34, 37, 43, 46
Combine subjects and predicates to construct sentences about familiar characters.	48, 49
Alphabetize words	32, 33, 35, 36, 38, 39
Write letters	53–55, 64, 65
Report	

Directions (North, South, East, West)

Follow directions involving **north** and **south**.	5–7
Follow directions involving **north, south, east, west**.	8, 9, 11, 14, 16, 22, 23
Fix up a map to show north **(N)**, south **(S)**, east **(E)**, west **(W)**	12, 13
Draw arrows to indicate **north, south, east, west.**	14
Use directions about **north, south, east, west** to solve a puzzle.	15, 16
Apply a directional rule to solve a maze.	18, 19
Identify the direction an arrow moves **from** and **to.**	23
Draw arrows to show movement **to** and **from** (**to** the east and **from** the west).	25, 27
Compose directions to show solutions to a map puzzle.	29, 32
Complete directions for going to different locations on a map.	54, 55
Apply a rule about moving south and north to a map of North America.	62

Dialect

Correcting	Edit words to **correct** a character's dialect.	6, 7, 14, 15, 24, 48
Creating and Discriminating	Write what a character says in a picture.	6
	Edit words to show a character's dialect.	8, 12, 13, 49, 57
	Make a picture consistent with details of a story by writing sentences that show dialect.	59
	Connect different assertions with the appropriate speaker.	68
	Write what a character is thinking in a picture.	69

Deductions

Objectives	Lessons
Say a deduction based on 3 pictures.	**8, 9**
Say different deductions based on pictures.	**11–15, 17, 22, 24, 38**
Construct deductions to answer questions.	**25, 28, 29, 44**
Identify the order of parts in a formally correct deduction.	**39**
Complete a deduction used in the story.	**52, 53**
Construct deductions that are formally incorrect.	**55**
Identify deductions that are formally correct (good) or incorrect.	**55**

Perspective

Relative Size	Edit a letter to show a character's reference to the relative sizes of objects.	**12**
	Identify speakers from references to the relative size of objects.	**16**
	Answer questions about relative size.	**18**
	Complete descriptions of relative size.	**19**
	Write a letter that contains descriptions of relative size.	**23**
Relative Direction	Complete descriptions involving relative direction.	**33–35**
	Identify where characters are on a map based on assertions about the direction of a common object.	**36, 38, 41, 43**
	Identify the characters on a map by their assertions about relative direction.	**46, 47**
	Complete statements of relative direction based on a map.	**56, 61, 62**
	Use rules about relative direction to indicate why specific places on a map are not the correct places.	**63**
	Write descriptions of "safe spots" based on rules about relative direction.	**64**

Temporal Sequencing

	Lessons
Complete sentences of the form: Blank happened after blank.	**27, 28, 34, 63**
Identify a specific picture sequence by applying clues about the order of actions shown.	**37, 39**
Write sentences that use the word after and tell what an illustrated character did.	**51–53, 63**
Write 2 clues for a mystery sequence.	**56**
Work cooperatively to write 2 clues for the mystery sequence.	**57**

Clarity

Correcting Ambiguity	Edit sentences to eliminate pronoun ambiguity.	**34, 35**
	Rewrite a passage so that it unambiguously reports on what a picture sequence shows.	**61**
	Edit sentences in a passage to eliminate ambiguity.	**62**
Creating Ambiguity	Rewrite unambiguous sentence pairs so the second sentence is ambiguous.	**47, 51, 54, 65**
Discriminating	Use cutouts to change specific details of a picture.	**36**
	Edit ambiguous sentences to show how a character interpreted them.	**37–39, 41–43, 45**
	Identify the illustrator of ambiguous sentences.	**55**

Reporting

Objectives	Lessons
Indicate whether statements about a picture **report** or **do not report**.	56, 57
Write sentences that report.	57–59

Story Grammar

	Objectives	Lessons
Model Stories	Answer comprehension questions about a story.	1–6, 11, 12, 15–17, 19, 21–26, 28, 29, 31–36, 38, 39, 41, 42, 48, 49, 51–53, 55–59, 61–
	Listen to a familiar story.	7–10, 13, 14, 18, 20, 27, 30, 37, 40, 43–47, 50, 54, 60
Application	Make a picture consistent with the details of a story.	1–5, 8, 9, 11, 17, 41, 42, 44, 53, 56, 65,
	Draw a picture based on a familiar story.	14
Extrapolation	Predict the outcome of a story.	23, 55
	Cooperatively compose an episode involving familiar story grammar.	27, 58
	Present a cooperatively-developed episode based on familiar story grammar.	28, 59
	Put on a play to show part of a familiar story.	47, 54

Part 2

The major tracks in Part 2 are:
>DEDUCTIONS
>SENTENCE ANALYSIS
>MECHANICS
>EDITING
>REPORTING—BASED ON PICTURES
>INFERRING
>CLARITY—BASED ON PICTURES

Within each track are divisions. Each division is marked by a subheading.

The subheadings for Sentence Analysis are:
>SUBJECT-PREDICATE
>VERBS
>PRONOUNS

The subheadings for Mechanics are:
>GENERAL
>CAPITALS AND ENDING MARKS
>APOSTROPHES

Deductions

Objectives	Lessons
Complete a simple deduction.	66–68
Draw conclusions based on different concrete examples.	69–71, 73, 77

Sentence Analysis

	Objectives	Lessons
Subject-Predicate	Identify the part of a sentence that names.	66–68
	Identify the part of a sentence that names (subject) and the part that tells more (predicate).	69–74, 84
	Indicate the subject of sentences in a paragraph.	76–81
	Indicate the subject and predicate of sentences.	86–90, 91, 93, 96
	Construct sentences by combining specific subjects and predicates.	90, 91, 97, 102
	Identify sentence parts as subjects or predicates.	98–100
	Identify the subject, predicate and verb in sentences.	106–108
Verbs	Change regular present-time verbs to past-time verbs by adding the suffix **e-d.**	69
	Write past-time verbs for irregular present-time verbs.	70, 71, 73, 76–79, 86–88, 90–94, 100–103, 107
	Change 2-word verbs in sentences to 1-word verbs.	71–74, 76, 78–81
	Change 2-word verbs in a paragraph to 1-word past-time verbs.	83, 84, 87
	Identify the verbs in sentences.	105
	Identify 2-word verbs.	109
	Identify the two actions specified in a sentence.	110
Pronouns	Replace the subject of a sentence with the appropriate pronoun (he, she, it or they).	72–74, 76–78, 97–99, 119
	Use appropriate pronouns in a short passage.	79–82, 89
	Use appropriate pronouns **(he, she** or **it)** in a paragraph.	90–94
	Determine whether it is appropriate to use a pronoun as the subject of a sentence.	106–108, 116–119

Mechanics

General	Follow conventions for using lined paper (numbers with periods before the margin, sentences with capitals and periods after the margin).	66, 67
	Copy item numbers and sentences onto lined paper.	68
	Copy a paragraph.	80–83
Capitals and Ending Marks	Punctuate sentences (capitals and periods) and identify the subject of the sentences in a paragraph.	82–84, 86–88
	Punctuate sentences (capitals and periods) in a paragraph.	89–91, 93, 94, 96, 97
	Capitalize the name of a person.	94
	Capitalize all parts of a person's name.	96–99
	Capitalize people's names in a paragraph.	100
Apostrophes	Rewrite expressions so that a word is written with an apostrophe **(the dress that belongs to the girl** becomes **the girl's dress).**	109, 110

Editing

Objectives	Lessons
Edit sentences for irregular past-time verbs.	95, 96, 98
Edit a paragraph for capitals, periods and past-time verbs.	98, 99, 104
Edit a paragraph for **he, she, it** and **they.**	100
Edit a paragraph for sentences that begin with **and** or **and then.**	101, 102, 104
Edit a paragraph to correct unclear parts.	101, 102, 104
Edit a paragraph for periods and capitals, including people's names.	102, 106
Edit run-on sentences.	104–106
Edit a paragraph for run-on sentences.	107–110

Reporting—Based on Pictures

Objectives	Lessons
Discriminate between sentences that report on a picture versus sentences that convey an inference.	66–69, 71, 72
Write appropriate subjects in sentences.	66–68
Construct sentences by combining given parts that name and parts that tell more.	69, 70
Select sentences that state the main thing that illustrated characters did.	71–73
Construct sentences that state the main thing that illustrated characters did.	74, 76–81
Select the appropriate name for a group.	80, 81
Select sentences that state the main thing that illustrated groups did.	82–84
Construct a paragraph that reports on what the members of an illustrated group did.	84–88
Write a sentence that states the main thing an illustrated group did.	86–89
Write two sentences about an illustrated character.	91, 92
Construct a paragraph that includes one sentence about an illustrated group and two sentences about each illustrated character.	93, 94, 96, 106
Write a paragraph that reports on an illustrated action sequence.	101–104

Clarity—Based on Pictures

Objectives	Lessons
Identify the set of pictures a sentence describes.	76–79, 82
Identify sentences that tell about all of the pictures, two of the pictures and one of the pictures.	88–90, 92
Complete similar sentences so they tell about only one picture.	93–96
Rewrite a paragraph to correct unclear parts.	97–100
Write a sentence that tells about only one of two similar pictures.	99, 100
Write a sentence that tells about only one of three similar pictures.	103, 104